Chopin

Unlocking the Masters Series, No. 11

Series Editor: Robert Levine

Chopin

A Listener's Guide to the Master of the Piano

Victor Lederer

AMADEUS
PRESS

Published in 2006 by Amadeus Press
512 Newark Pompton Turnpike
Pompton Plains, New Jersey 07444

Book design by Snow Creative Services

Printed in the United States of America

Library of Congress Cataloging-in-Publication Data is available upon request.

ISBN 1-57467-148-0

www.amadeuspress.com

For my wife, with love and gratitude

Contents

Acknowledgments

Thanks to my children, Paul and Karen, for their encouragement through the process of developing and writing this book, and for putting up with a constant stream of Chopin—often the same piece over and over—for six months.

I confess to the possession of a secret weapon: my piano teacher and friend, Bernard Rose. One of New York's great pianists, musicians, and teachers, Bernie's profound understanding of the technical aspects of Chopin's music and his warmhearted approach to music making were indispensable in helping me see Chopin's aesthetic goals and the remarkable daring of so much of what he wrote. Bernie was ready, willing, and able to play through music he had not touched for years: an impromptu read-through for me of the F minor Ballade one afternoon lingers in my memory as extraordinary and surpassingly moving. Studying with Bernie over the last few years has raised my comprehension of musical structure immeasurably: I have learned from him the wide gulf between listening passively—no matter how closely and lovingly—and hearing music as a practicing musician.

This book could and would not exist without the help of my editor and dear friend, Bob Levine. His own love for and deep knowledge of music, as well as his electric wit, make him constantly exciting and fun to work with. Bob's experience in critical writing is so broad and his instincts so fine that I found myself questioning everything he questioned and agreeing readily with all of his suggestions: often enough Bob knew what I trying to say before I could get my own thoughts out coherently. Bob's role was much more that of colleague—and even collaborator—than that of a normal editor.

Chopin

Chopin's Brief Life and Long Death

C hopin's life is rich with contradictions. Born of humble stock, he was fully aware of his own worth, carrying himself regally with manners learned from the Polish and Russian aristocrats who pampered him as a child prodigy. Although Chopin is considered one of the greatest pianists in history, his fame as a performer is based on no more than thirty public appearances, some of which were given in the small Parisian recital hall of the French piano manufacturer Pleyel; nor was his playing at all like the thundering of most virtuosos. Slight and frail, Chopin relied instead on infinitely graded volume and expressive shading that grew subtler as tuberculosis weakened him. A foolish legend paints the illness as a condition of his moonlit romantic genius, but in fact it caused him terrible suffering and deprived him of several productive years before killing him. One of the most famous piano teachers in the Paris of the 1830s and '40s, Chopin had no pupils of consequence and, unlike his friend Liszt, fathered no school of piano playing. His long relationship with the eccentric, cross-dressing, cigar-smoking writer George Sand (a woman whose real name was Aurore Dudevant) is well documented but seems curiously out of character for the reserved, conservative Chopin. Documents from his early life reveal a normal if supremely gifted youth who grew more unhappy and difficult as the twinned demands of illness and genius tightened their grip on him.

Chopin's paradoxes, like those of most people, began with his parents. His father, Nicholas, a native of Lorraine in northeastern France, came from a family of poor farmers. But the quick-minded Nicholas caught the attention of the Polish administrator of a large estate, with whom the sixteen-year-old moved to Poland in 1787. From that moment, Nicholas, who worked as a clerk and French tutor to various noble families, turned his back on France, apparently dropping all contact with his family. He adopted his new country with a vengeance, even joining the National Guard and, in 1806, marrying Justyna Krzyzanowski, from a poor but respectable family. Nicholas and Justyna Chopin produced four children: Ludwika in 1807; Frédéric on March 1, 1810; Isabella in 1811; and Emilia in 1812.

The tale so far is the fairly normal one of an émigré. But a curious fact lurks in the background: this French native who tutored French for a living spoke only Polish at home. For Frédéric, French was always a second language and evidently one he never fully mastered, even after living in France for two decades. One has to wonder why Nicholas failed to teach his own children what was the most widely accepted symbol of gentility in Europe of the time, particularly among the middle and upper classes of Poland and Russia. For a man as alert and upwardly mobile as Nicholas Chopin appears to have been—not to mention one who would have found it easy to teach his children French—he consciously deprived them of a crucial social skill. This inexplicable issue of language is a fault line in Chopin's early life. His complete identification as a Pole is of course the world's gain, but given the circumstances, it seems strange that he grew up without the least sense of being part French.

In 1810, when Frédéric was born, the Chopin family lived in a pretty but primitive cottage in Zelazowa Wola, a small town west of Warsaw; the house stands today. All four of the Chopin children appear to have been gifted, and music was always part of life in the home, with Nicholas playing the violin and flute and Justyna the piano. It is worth noting that the Chopins owned a piano in the years before mass production put one in every European home with aspirations of culture. Frédéric showed a powerful pull toward music at an early age, weeping at the sound of his mother's playing, according to one story. At age four, he became a pupil of his mother and older sister; by six he had mastered all they could teach, playing works far beyond the capacity of a normal child of his age and beginning to improvise. By age seven, his parents placed him with Adalbert Zywyny, a Czech pianist, violinist, and composer. That Nicholas and Justyna nurtured their son's prodigious gift shows them unmistakably to have been tender and solicitous parents.

Chopin was fortunate in his two music teachers. Neither Zywny nor Joseph Elsner, who later taught him at the Warsaw Conservatory, made the slightest attempt to deflect the trajectory of a genius that manifested itself early and overwhelmingly. Zywny gave Chopin a good grounding in the fundamentals of music, introducing him to the works of Bach and Mozart, who became his musical gods, as well as to Haydn's compositions and those of the lesser pianist-composers Johann Nepomuk Hummel and Ferdinand Ries. By 1817 Chopin had begun to play in public and compose. The inevitable comparisons with the child prodigy Mozart were drawn: fame had come to the composer that would stay with him for the rest of his life. It was in that year that Chopin gave his debut performance, as soloist in a concerto, and that his first composition, a short polonaise, was published. A Warsaw reviewer wrote:

> The composer of this dance, only eight years of age, is a real musical genius. . . . He not only performs the most difficult pieces on the piano with the greatest ease and extraordinary taste, but is also the composer of several dances and variations that fill the experts with amazement. . . . May the present notice also remind readers that geniuses are born in our country also.

The public exposure brought Chopin to the attention—and admiration—of the Polish aristocracy. They immediately took him under their wing, bringing him to their palaces to perform. From an early age, Chopin socialized constantly with the nobility and grew up with their children, putting him into contact with the manners, speech, and dress of those in the highest tier of society. He also came to the attention of Grand Duke Constantine Pavlovich, ruler of Poland and brother of the Tsar of Russia. Since 1772 Poland had been under the domination of its three powerful neighbors: Russia, Austria, and Prussia (the kingdom that was the chief forerunner of Germany). By 1795, the three had swallowed Poland completely, with Russia in possession of Warsaw and the Polish heartland when Chopin was born. Carved up repeatedly after wars, Poland seethed with an ineffectual desire for independence, manifested by periodic revolts, all brutally repressed: a background crucial to Chopin's emotional life and musical development.

Hated by the Poles, Constantine seems to have suffered from bipolar disorder or, more likely, full-blown schizophrenia, sometimes rampaging through Warsaw with a rifle and then sinking into spirits so low that he could not leave his room. At these times, Chopin—already the pride of Poland—was brought to his palace to play for him, evidently succeeding to some degree in calming the Grand Duke's troubled mind. In 1818, the young prodigy played for the Dowager Empress Maria Fedorovna, mother of Constantine and his brother, Tsar Alexander I, for whom Chopin would perform in 1825.

Chopin's parents enrolled him in 1823 in the Warsaw Lyceum, a secondary school where his musical education for a few years took second place to the Greek, Latin, classics, and mathematics that were the standard academic fare of the period. But Chopin spent several of these summers in his birthplace of Zelazowa Wola, where he heard—and danced—the mazurka in its infinite variety. The Chopin of this period was by all accounts a cheerful, outgoing boy: a gifted mimic and more or less regular fellow who displayed none of the haughty reserve he would later be known for. Small but physically active, he performed enthusiastically in theatrical productions in school and at home, skated in the winter, and listened with the keenest pleasure to peasant songs and dances on his summer vacations in the countryside outside Warsaw.

In June of 1825, Chopin played an organlike contraption called the Aeolomelodikon for Tsar Alexander I on a visit to Warsaw, receiving a gold ring as a gift from the emperor. Soon after, Chopin's first commercially published composition, the Rondo in C minor, op. 1, was issued. The rondo is one of the few of Chopin's published works that is rarely heard today, but it was well received by the musical press of the day.

In 1826 Chopin began his studies at the Warsaw Conservatory under Joseph Elsner, an academic and composer with whom he had been studying privately for over a year. The conservatory program for students of composition included the writing of a vast range of forms, from masses to chamber works, which Chopin seems to have slogged through dutifully, if without enthusiasm. Chopin's Piano Sonata no. 1, op. 4, is a product of his time at the conservatory. Dedicated to Elsner, the work contains some bold and interesting ideas. Elsner, who clearly grasped the magnitude of his pupil's gift, seems not to have leaned on him, and all existing documents show a high mutual regard between him and Chopin.

In 1829 Elsner wrote about Chopin in the school register: "Third year student, outstanding abilities; musical genius." Another story reveals Elsner's astute judgment and flexibility. When asked by colleagues why he let Chopin experiment with the rules of composition, he is said to have replied, "Leave him in peace. His is an extraordinary path, for he has an extraordinary gift. He does not follow the old rules because he seeks those of his own." Chopin repaid the compliment when asked how he had learned so much in provincial Warsaw by saying, evidently with some heat, that "with Messers Zywny and Elsner even the greatest jackass would have learned." Struggling to explain Chopin's extraordinary synergy with the piano, scholars have recently tried, with little success, to name a third teacher who at least got him going on the instrument. But the astonishing truth about Chopin is that as a pianist, he seems to have been largely self-taught: Zywny was a violinist who also played the piano, and Elsner a theoretician and composer. Chopin, the greatest composer for the piano and one of the two or three greatest pianists ever to play the instrument, figured it out for himself. Born to play and compose, he was a freak of nature and one of history's great geniuses.

During this period, Chopin began to display physical frailty with constant colds and respiratory infections; in April 1827, his youngest sister Emilia died at fourteen of tuberculosis, a major world-health problem until the mid-twentieth century and the illness that would eventually fell Chopin. It was around this time that Chopin wrote the earliest of his works that is performed regularly: the mature and darkly beautiful Nocturne in E minor, published only after his death. Early in 1828, he met the famous pianist and composer Johann Nepomuk Hummel, on tour in Warsaw. Although thirty years older than Chopin, Hummel recognized in the younger artist another keyboard giant, and the two swiftly became good friends. The musical world outside of

Warsaw also made itself felt in Chopin's life when Robert Schumann wrote of Chopin the famous phrase "Hats off, gentlemen, a genius!" in his review of Chopin's Variations for Piano and Orchestra on *Là ci darem la mano*.

That Warsaw—in no sense a musical capital—was far too small an arena for his talents as composer and pianist must have been painfully evident to Chopin by this time. He made his first journey as a mature artist seeking his place in the musical universe to Berlin in September 1828. There he took in many operatic and choral performances. Vocal music, particularly opera, remained Chopin's passion throughout his life. In May of 1829, the great violinist Niccolo Paganini visited Warsaw, astounding Chopin, as he did everyone who heard him play, with a virtuosity that exceeded that of any violinist before—and quite possibly since. Chopin quickly came to want to exploit the resources of the piano as Paganini had done with the violin, making it produce effects that were new and daring but still completely idiomatic to the instrument. In the end, Chopin's success exceeded that of Liszt, who sought to imbue in many of his own works the spirit of Paganini's virtuosity and even that of Paganini himself, because he was a far greater composer than either. It was after hearing Paganini that Chopin began work on his first set of *etudes* (studies), which remain the greatest works since those of Bach to blend specific technical problems with the highest artistry.

By 1830 Chopin could no longer put off leaving Poland to seek his artistic fortune in the greater European stage. That autumn he left for Vienna, home base for many years of the giants Haydn, Mozart, Beethoven, and Schubert, and surely the city with the richest musical heritage. He had visited the Austrian capital over the summer of 1829, making friends—including Beethoven's pupil Carl Czerny and patron, Prince Lichnowsky—among the Viennese social and musical aristocracy, and performing his *Là ci darem* Variations in a wildly successful concert. But this second visit was a different, far less happy affair for the young composer. In Vienna, Chopin was just one among many fine pianists: facing a surfeit of talent, the Viennese were both demanding and indifferent, quite unlike the reliably adulatory Warsaw community. Tobias Haslinger, the Viennese publisher who had printed the *Là ci darem* Variations on speculation, remained friendly but firmly unwilling to take up Chopin's cause again, presumably having lost money on the first venture. The critics also complained about the small tone of Chopin's playing.

Chopin attempted to leave for Paris, but as a Russian subject, he had great difficulty in obtaining permission from that nation's embassy in Vienna to leave. At last he was allowed to go; passing through Munich and Stuttgart in early 1831, Chopin learned of the insurrection against the Russians that had begun in Warsaw a month after his departure from the city and been swiftly and savagely crushed by vastly larger forces. The entries in Chopin's journal from these weeks consist of long, furious rants that reflect his fear for his family and friends, many of whom were deeply involved in the revolt. It is at this time that Chopin's feeling for his suffering homeland seems to have refocused his music powerfully, bringing the series of cheerful variations on operatic or Polish themes to an end, and initiating the series of grippingly dark polonaises and haunting mazurkas that would occupy him for the rest of his life and mark his work with a nationalism that no composer had yet attempted.

Chopin arrived in Paris in early October of 1831. The city was the center of Western cultural life, with many important composers, including Rossini, Berlioz, and Liszt; writers, such as Stendhal, Victor Hugo and Balzac; and the great painter Eugene Delacroix at the heart of its mighty ferment. Social activity in artistic circles was organized around *salons,* evening gatherings in the homes of the creators or their patrons where new music was played, manuscripts read aloud, politics argued, and champagne drunk. Intellectual merit carried all the weight at these assemblies, with wealthy merchants and aristocrats vying for the privilege of presenting men and women of talent in their own homes.

Rather like New York in the twentieth century, Paris was also the destination for the dispossessed of Europe, including thousand of Polish nobles, intellectuals, and revolutionaries who fled their motherland in the wake of the failed rebellion of 1830. Chopin immediately joined the ranks of the Parisian musical community, all of whom seem to have recognized their new acquaintance's genius from the beginning. Various efforts were made to get Chopin's career on track, including a proposal from Fredrich Kalkbrenner—a famous pianist of the time, much admired by Chopin—that the young Pole devote the next three years (and considerable expense) to studying with Kalkbrenner. At the receiving end of torrents of advice from his family and teacher Elsner back home, Chopin vacillated before finally declining the offer, heeding his new friend Felix Mendelssohn's opinion that he was already a far greater pianist than Kalkbrenner.

Chopin was introduced to the Parisian public at a concert in February 1832, where, in a program typical for the era, he shared the billing with a number of other instrumentalists, including pianists and string players, as well as singers. Chopin's generous friend and colleague Franz Liszt, who was present at the concert, wrote, attempting to catch the originality of Chopin's music and the richness and delicacy of his playing: "The most vociferous applause was insufficient for the talent that was opening a new phase in poetic sentiment and presenting happy innovations in the substance of his art." The review of the concert by the musicologist and critic Francois Joseph Fétis was more articulate:

> Here is a young man who, surrendering himself to his natural impressions and taking no model, has found, if not a complete renewal of piano music, at least a part of that which we have long sought in vain, namely an abundance of original ideas of a kind to be found nowhere else. I find in M. Chopin's inspirations the signs of a renewal of forms which may henceforth exercise considerable influence.

The sound of Chopin's music, distinctive and inimitable, and the incomparable beauty of his playing made it clear from the start that he was perhaps the greatest musical talent among the many gifted musicians working in Paris.

Temperamentally unsuited to the strains that have always accompanied the life of a performing artist in need of a steady income, Chopin began to teach. His pupils came chiefly from the ranks of the wealthy and well born, mainly the wives and daughters of bankers and princes, although all seem to have been serious, hard-working amateurs; he did not accept beginners or children as pupils. There were also a few professional pianists, not one of whom went on to a major career as a performer. Chopin quickly became the most fashionable piano teacher in Paris, charging an exorbitant 20 francs per lesson. This equals about perhaps $75 or $80 in today's money, which although high does not sound extravagant—and certainly cheap for an hour of Chopin's time—but one should consider that the average French laborer of the day earned 5 or 6 francs a week.

"You think I am making a fortune?" he wrote. "Carriages and white gloves cost more, and without them one would not be *bon ton* [in good taste]." Much has been made biographically of Chopin's dandyism and spendthrift ways, but by every account, he was an extraordinary teacher, passionately dedicated to sharing his transcendent technique and matchless feel for the piano. Many of Chopin's students wrote memoirs of their time with him; these agree almost universally that although his standards were high and he was difficult to please, he was also profoundly encouraging and inspiring.

Chopin preferred to give lessons at his own apartment, although when healthy (as he often was not, especially toward the end of his life), he was willing to teach at the student's, but he had to be picked up and driven home afterward. The student was to leave the 20-franc payment on his mantelpiece. Chopin, meticulous in his dress and grooming, was always well turned out. This busy man, aware of the value of his time, insisted that his pupils be prompt, although lessons frequently ran longer than the scheduled hour, especially when no other appointment followed. Chopin had the student play at his Pleyel grand piano, while he might sit, stand, or pace the room; he also accompanied and illustrated from a smaller instrument, which he did often, and often at great length. He gave the student his absolute attention. One recalled: "Chopin was a born teacher; expression and conception, position of the hands, touch, pedaling, nothing escaped the sharpness of his hearing and his vision; he gave every detail the keenest attention. Entirely absorbed in his task, during the lessons he would be solely a teacher and nothing but a teacher."

Piano students today would do well to consider the reports of Chopin's methods and priorities. According to a colleague, he advised his students to "have the body supple, right to the tips of the toes." Carl Mikuli, a pupil who later edited Chopin's works, recalled that

"Chopin's main concern was to do away with every stiffness and convulsive or cramped movement of the hand, in order to facilitate the primary requisite of good playing: suppleness, and with it independence of the fingers." He asked his pupils to make the piano—a percussion instrument inside which hammers hit strings—sing, advising them to use the great Italian vocalists as their models. He detested exaggeration of any sort, demanding a simplicity and naturalness in his students' playing.

He was also one of the first piano teachers who instinctually understood the danger of practicing mechanically and for too long a period. Chopin believed that practicing required the student's full attention and will, that three hours' practicing a day was the maximum advisable, and that breaks to refresh the body and mind were imperative. Although demanding with every student and impatient with the lazy ones, Chopin often displayed great enthusiasm and was profoundly insightful about each pupil's style of learning. One wrote:

> To encourage me, he tells me. . . . "It seems to me that you don't dare express yourself as you feel. Be bolder, let yourself go more. . . . Forget you're being listened to and always listen to yourself. I see that timidity and lack of self-confidence form a kind of armor around you, but through this armor I perceive something else that you don't dare to express, and so you deprive us all.

Another student's story reveals the preternatural sensitivity of Chopin's ear as well as the absolute attention he paid to his students. Late in Chopin's life, tuberculosis had weakened him to the point where he often taught lying down on the couch in the room adjoining his music studio.

> But this did not prevent him from attentively following her playing; even from a distance, and out of sight, not the slightest detail of her playing escaped him. "Fourth finger on F-sharp," he would call out; his ear, sensitive to the slightest nuance, knew immediately, from the sound, which finger had played each note.

Chopin began work on an instructional document that he called "Sketch for a Method." Although he didn't get too far, the document is invaluable in helping listeners understand Chopin's philosophy of music and piano playing. It also reveals his clarity of thought and suggests his excellence as a pedagogue. Referring to the fact that unlike string instruments, which performers themselves tune and then *play* in tune, the piano is regulated by a technician, Chopin wrote:

> Intonation being the tuner's task, the piano is free of one of the greatest difficulties encountered in the study of an instrument. . . . One needs only to study a certain positioning of the hand in relation to the keys to obtain with ease the most beautiful quality of sound, to know how to play long notes and short notes, and to attain unlimited dexterity.

In addition to technical studies by Clementi and Cramer, which are still standard fare for piano students today, Chopin taught compositions by Beethoven, Schubert, Weber, Scarlatti, and Mendelssohn. Chopin shared with all musicians a reverence for Bach, whom he taught constantly and studied carefully himself. He sometimes taught his own works, especially the nocturnes. It is easy to imagine the mixture of anxiety and dizzy anticipation his students felt when playing these masterpieces for their creator or hearing one of the great geniuses in the history of music demonstrating how to play them. That experience would be extraordinary, if not positively apocalyptic, for any music lover; for many it was indeed overwhelming, and there are numerous accounts of Chopin's pupils weeping after hearing their teacher play.

For the most sensitive of Chopin's disciples, everyday life must have seemed particularly gray and pointless after hearing the master perform his music, privately and peerlessly, just for them. Clearly Chopin's own keyboard mastery was awe-inspiring to his fellow musicians, who were unanimous in placing him in his own class, far beyond praise. His matchless fluidity and expressiveness induced trancelike states in himself and his listeners. Ferdinand Hiller, an eminent pianist and friend of Chopin's, commented:

> His wonderful playing will remain impressed on my soul until I draw my last breath. . . . I have said that he rarely opened his heart, but at the piano he abandoned himself more completely than any other musician I have ever heard—with such concentration that all extraneous thoughts fell away.

Charles Hallé, a German-born pianist whose career was chiefly in England, wrote:

> the same evening I heard—*Chopin*. That was beyond all words.
> The few senses I had have quite left me. . . . Everything I hear now
> seems so insignificant that I would rather not hear it at all. Chopin!
> He is no man, he is an angel. . . . Chopin's compositions played by
> Chopin! That is a joy never to be surpassed.

In his autobiography, written years later, Hallé added to his reminiscence of that evening: "I could only stammer a few broken words of admiration, and he played again and again, each time revealing new beauties, until I could have dropped on my knees to worship him." Such was the transcendent nature of Chopin's playing and its effect on others.

Franz Liszt, the German composer of Hungarian descent, was Chopin's contemporary, colleague, and perhaps only equal as a pianist. But their styles of playing were as different as their personalities. They shared a troubled friendship that began when Chopin arrived in Paris in 1830 and limped on until Chopin's death. The difficulties seem to have been chiefly on Chopin's side: Liszt never expressed anything but reverence for Chopin as a composer and pianist. He played Chopin's works regularly and by every account with the greatest brilliance.

A handsome six-footer, Liszt had a physical strength and stamina that far surpassed that of the frail Chopin. Liszt dazzled audiences (especially women, who threw themselves at him) with a technique at the piano the like of which had never been heard, including effects where the instrument was made to sound like a full orchestra. Chopin's playing—refined, ethereal, and songful—could not compete with Liszt's electricity; sensibly, Chopin did not try. Their coexistence in the same time and place is one of those curious pairings of giants in musical history.

Although most listeners and critics understood that Chopin's marvelous playing had to be taken on its own terms, it was also noted, and accepted, that he lacked the strength to play loudly. Chopin was openly envious of Liszt's easy dominance of the Parisian musical scene and his power at the piano. He wrote to Ferdinand Hiller "Liszt is playing my etudes and transporting me outside of my respectable thoughts. I should like to steal from him the way to play my own etudes." Liszt's gregarious, sometimes flamboyant personality seems at times to have disgusted Chopin, who himself grew more reserved and ironic as time passed. And he had no use for Liszt's compositions, such as the Hungarian rhapsodies or the reductions of favorite operatic moments to virtuoso fantasies for the piano.

For the next few years, Chopin grew rich teaching fashionable Paris, giving a few public performances, and composing in the inimitable style that made all but the most reactionary listeners realize that he was one of the leading figures of European music. In 1832 he met and became friends with Hector Berlioz, one of the leaders of those radical musicians broadly referred to as the romantics. Chopin's music is usually grouped with that of Liszt, Berlioz, Schumann, and the other composers of the early romantic era, but he himself repudiated their work and goals. Conservative in his tastes (and politics), Chopin stood apart from his colleagues in many ways, although he and Berlioz seem to have enjoyed a solid friendship.

Vincenzo Bellini, the great Italian opera composer, also lived in Paris, and he and Chopin became friends. Chopin had the deepest admiration for Bellini's ability to spin endless melodies for his singers, and Chopin mastered the art of writing such tunes for the piano—although he adapted Bellini's style, in which the limitations of the human voice were of course a key element, to the piano, where a wider range of notes was possible. Perhaps the two most obvious examples of "Bellinian" melodies in Chopin are the Nocturne in D-flat major, op. 27, no. 2 (track 8 on the CD at the back of the book), and the first movement of the Sonata no. 3 in B minor, op. 58, but there are countless others as well. Although Chopin was, despite his conservative tastes and tendencies, one of the great revolutionaries in the history of Western music, and Bellini a towering figure in the more tradition-bound forms of Italian opera, the two musicians shared a profound feeling for memorable, singable melody. Both were also outsiders in France (Bellini was Sicilian), and ultimately, both died there prematurely, Chopin at thirty-nine and Bellini at thirty-four.

Chopin made the acquaintance of the author George Sand, the pen name of Amandine Aurore Lucille Dupin Dudevant, in the autumn of

1836. Sand, a prolific author as well as a major figure in the cultural life of Paris of the period, was descended on her father's side from a clan of some distinction with ties to the Bourbons, the royal family of France. Her father, Maurice, was a soldier in Napoleon's army in Milan when he stole Antionette Delaborde, a dancer and the mistress of a French general, from her protector. Antoinette's parents seem to have been a carpenter and a Parisian street vendor, making her background far different from that of her lover. They had two children, of whom Aurore was the second.

Maurice Dupin died young, and Antionette paid only sporadic attention to Aurore, who was raised at her ancestral home (on the paternal side) in Nohant, a small town in the remote central French province of Berry. There she was tutored well, reading everything she could get her hands on. Aurore also grew up as an outdoorswoman, hunting, riding, and learning how to run her family estate. Married young to the Baron Casimir Dudevant, an old-line aristocrat of no discernable talent or quality of character, Aurore soon found herself chafing against her unhappy situation and the institution of marriage in general.

In 1831 her passionate, impulsive spirit rebelled. Taking her two young children with her, she moved to Paris, where she at first worked as a journalist and then began writing the long series of novels and plays that made her famous and, in some circles, notorious. Using her own experience as inspiration, Sand generally cranked out more than one long novel every year. These were immensely popular, particularly with women, and were immediately translated into English. Although her books were daring for their time, they are now mainly of sociohistorical interest and remain mostly unread; the best known today is probably *Léila,* published in 1833. Sand had a powerful sexual drive, and much of what she wrote dealt with sex in its various guises. Smoking cigars and dressing at times as a man, Sand took many lovers over the years, flaunting them in the face of the conservative elements of French society, but remained a member in good standing of the Paris salon circle.

Chopin's affair with Sand was from early 1837 until 1845, although it seems likely that their physical relationship lasted only for the first year or two. Temperamentally they could not have been more different. Sand was of a domineering and magnetic personality: independent, outgoing, and politically liberal. Chopin, a reactionary in his very limited politics, carried himself with a reserve that was aristocratic and even regal. A memoir by the pianist Wilhelm von Lenz provides a fascinating look at Chopin's manner with a stranger: "Chopin came to greet me—a young man of medium height, slender, lanky, his face worn and expressive and his dress of the greatest Paris refinement.... Chopin did not invite me to sit down and I remained standing, as in the presence of a sovereign." Lenz, who had a letter of introduction from Liszt, played for Chopin, who took him on as a pupil, saying, "All right, I'll give you lessons, but only twice a week, that's my maximum; it will be hard for me to find three-quarters of an hour."

Sand and Chopin first met at a gathering on the evening of October 24, 1836. As with most of her lovers, Sand was the seducer; like most of her men, Chopin was younger, romantically passive. He was also in poor health, already suffering constantly from respiratory problems—perhaps the tuberculosis that ultimately killed him. Chopin's first impression of Sand, who dressed that night in men's clothing, reflected a horrified fascination: "What an unsympathetic woman! Is she really a woman? I almost doubt it," Chopin said, according to Ferdinand Hiller, who rode home with him that evening. But Sand, who was herself musical, had fallen in love with Chopin and his playing. And so she persisted, wearing the Polish colors in the form of a white gown with a red sash and staring soulfully at the composer when he played at other soirees. Chopin was gradually conquered over the course of the following months. After a dinner on April 25, 1838, Sand sent Chopin a note that said "One adores you!—George!" Sand understood the magnitude of Chopin's gifts. They never married, and the arrangement between them was entirely modern: they lived and traveled together as a couple for the next nine years.

An intrepid tourist at a time when travel was always uncomfortable and often dangerous, Sand jumped when her physician suggested that a warm climate would help the rheumatism of her son, Maurice. Chopin, too, hoped to alleviate his own growing discomforts by getting away from the long, cold Northern European winter. They settled on Majorca, the Spanish island in the Western Mediterranean, for which they set out in October 1838 with high expectations.

When Chopin, Sand, and Sand's children, Maurice and Solange, arrived, the warm autumn weather, the subtropical foliage, and the local music accompanied by guitar enchanted the travelers. What they liked far less were their miserable accommodations in a community that received few outsiders, and the suspicion and hostility with which the natives treated them. Finally, they rented space in Valldemosa, an abandoned and partially ruined monastery about eight miles outside Palma, Majorca's capital and main city. No sooner were Chopin, Sand, and her tribe settled in when the weather turned, with sharp changes in temperature and winter rains sweeping the island. The damp settled into the walls of the monastery, a structure far more primitive than any Sand and Chopin were used to, and with it a chill that would not dissipate. Chopin suffered terribly from respiratory problems worse than those he experienced in Paris, but without Parisian medical care. Additionally, the entire group found the rustic, greasy, garlicky food inedible. Sand, whose maternal instincts seem to have been as powerful as her sex drive, took over the cooking of every meal, taught her children every morning, wrote every night, and cared for Chopin, whose condition deteriorated alarmingly nonetheless.

What is remarkable is how productive Chopin was in Majorca, composing, despite his illness, many works and completing many already in progress. Biographies of creative giants inevitably dwell on facts of the lives of great men and women, often making a run at analyzing the suffering in the act of creation, but few seem to take into account their steely will and self-discipline. Composing was Chopin's work, and compose he did, no matter how miserable the conditions or how sick he was. For Chopin, the act of creation was brutally difficult, not for lack of ideas, but for the work in shaping these into forms that satisfied the composer, as Sand saw and described:

> His music was spontaneous, miraculous. He found it without seeking it, without previous intimation of it. . . . But then began the most desperate labor that I have ever witnessed. It was a succession of efforts, hesitations, and moments of impatience to recapture certain details of the theme he could hear; what he had conceived as one piece, he analyzed too much in trying to write

down, and his dismay at his inability to rediscover it in what he thought was its original purity threw him into a kind of despair. He would lock himself up in his room for whole days, weeping, pacing back and forth, breaking his pens, repeating or changing one bar a hundred times, writing and erasing it as many times, and beginning again the next day with an infinite and desperate perseverance. He sometimes spent six weeks on one page, only in the end to write it exactly as he had sketched at the first draft.

Eugene Delacroix, the great painter and perhaps Chopin's closest friend (he called Chopin "the truest artist I ever met"), was himself more than familiar with the agonizing work of creation. Writing trenchantly about one of his long conversations about music with Chopin, Delacroix observed:

> Art is not what the common herd imagine it to be—a sort of inspiration from I-know-not-where, something proceeding from chance and portraying merely the picturesque exterior of things. It is reason itself, adorned by genius but following a course determined and restrained by superior laws.

That Chopin found the strength to compose in poor health and despite the miserable conditions at Valldemosa testifies to the immeasurable force of creative energy within the man.

But by mid-February of 1839, Chopin's condition and mood had deteriorated so badly that he, Sand, and her children had to leave. By this time Chopin was desperately ill, coughing up large quantities of blood, which suggests that tuberculosis had taken firm hold in his system. After a miserable voyage to Barcelona, in which the travelers shared the boat with a load of pigs, Chopin arrived more dead than alive. In that civilized city, he at last received good medical care and rallied. Deciding to stay south for the remainder of the winter, Chopin and Sand moved to Marseilles, where they remained until May 1839. Finally able to consume palatable food, Chopin grew stronger in the mild Provençal climate. In early June, he returned with the Sand family to Nohant.

Tuberculosis is a bacterial infection that was a major killer throughout the nineteenth and first half of the twentieth centuries; Chopin's, which he probably picked up in his early or middle twenties, seems to have settled in his larynx. There was no cure at the time. Images of Chopin coughing discreetly into his handkerchief while wasting gently away in the moonlight are rubbish. He suffered an agonizing suffocation over the course of years, spending longer and longer trying to clear his throat and lungs every morning before he felt he could breathe freely, until finally that moment never came. References to breathing are frequent in his pre-1840 letters and to choking and suffocation almost continual afterward. Good physicians of the mid-nineteenth century could do little more than palliate their patient's suffering, and not much of that. Thus, while Chopin recovered from his Majorcan illness, he was on an irrevocable course toward an awful death ten years later.

Chopin and Sand spent that summer in Nohant, finally returning to Paris in the fall. With their time divided unequally between Paris and Nohant, Chopin and Sand now occupied the center of Parisian cultural life, which was at a rarely matched high point of intellectual richness and ferment. They counted as close friends the cream of the artistic community, including Delacroix, Elizabeth Barrett Browning, Victor Hugo, Honoré de Balzac, Heinrich Heine, Stendhal, Berlioz, Charles Gounod, Mendelssohn, Liszt (whose friendship with Chopin had cooled somewhat), the eccentric pianist-composer Charles-Valentin Alkan, and the Spanish soprano Pauline Viardot, who was particularly beloved by both Chopin and Sand. Many of Chopin's Polish friends, all refugees from their homeland, were regulars at their social gatherings, as were members of the Rothschild family, several of whom were Chopin's pupils.

Despite his weakening health, the next several years were a golden era for Chopin, with one masterpiece following another. His rate of production dropped as his perfectionism grew, however, and he continued to teach daily and concertize infrequently. Like many of the greatest musicians, Chopin had a longstanding loathing and dread of performing in public. When he did play, it was in the small auditorium in the Pleyel showroom, to an invited audience and for a huge fee. (Chopin earned a great deal of money but was habitually improvident). Berlioz wrote:

He comes down from the clouds once a year and allows himself to be heard in Pleyel's salons, and only then the public and the artists can admire his magnificent talent. The rest of the year—unless one is a prince, minister, or ambassador—it is difficult to dream about the joy of hearing him.

Except for the occasional complaint that he did not play loudly enough, Chopin was viewed by this time as being in his own class, beyond criticism and praise, as two reviews of a concert he gave on April 26, 1841, at the Salle Pleyel show. The writer from *La Revue Musicale* commented that "Chopin has broken new trails for himself. His playing and his composition, from the very beginning, have won such high standing that in the eyes of many he has become an inexplicable phenomenon." The reviewer from *La France Musicale* wrote: "Nothing equals the lightness and sweetness of his preluding on the piano, nothing compares with his works in originality, distinction and grace. Chopin is unique as a pianist—he should not and cannot be compared with anyone."

Capitalizing on his popularity, Liszt was the first pianist to play the kind of solo concert that is now called a recital. Typical musical events of the early and middle nineteenth century involved different soloists—including one or more pianist, vocalists, violinists, and a small orchestra—with the individual sections of concertos or symphonies interspersed with short performances by the various soloists. Chopin's concerts took a middle path between the seriousness of a Liszt-style solo recital and the relaxed, often circuslike atmosphere of a mixed concert. A typical one might open with Chopin playing four or five of his own compositions, followed by him accompanying a singer (Pauline Viardot was a favorite colleague) in some art songs or an aria from an opera. Viardot sometimes sang wordless vocal lines to Chopin's own mazurkas, a practice to which he obviously had no objection, as he played the accompaniment. Following a break, Chopin played a few more solo pieces, after which another soloist would join him in an intimate chamber piece for piano and violin or cello. One of Chopin's closest friends was the cellist August Franchomme, who played with the composer often and whose soulful virtuosity was the stimulus for Chopin to compose the Sonata for Piano and Cello, op. 65.

The relationship between Chopin and Sand had changed. Having cared for the ailing composer in Majorca, Sand was now more mother than lover, fretting over Chopin's health and eating habits and acting as promoter for his rare performances. References to Chopin in Sand's letters use the sort of diminutive nicknames bestowed by a parent on a child, "Frik-Frik" and "Chip-Chip"; she also called him "angel," "the boy" or "my boy," "the poor child," and occasionally even "my son." Chopin appeared to adore Sand but grew more depressed, moody, and withdrawn as the months passed. His regal reserve turned into an ironic chilliness; sometimes he refused to speak to Sand for days without telling her the cause of his anger.

With pupils, his temper frayed quickly and hard. Zofia Rosengardt, a young Pole who came to Paris to study with Chopin in 1844, described him as "excessively polite . . . cold . . . indifferent . . . proud, weird and incomprehensible . . . petulant . . . evil and angry." There is no clear explanation why, except perhaps that his throat and lungs troubled him more all the time and that his heroic hard work was starting to exact a toll as well. But there is surely no hint of decay or exhaustion in his works from the early 1840s, which, if anything, show Chopin's genius at flood tide.

While Sand may have grown as weary of caring for Chopin as she was of dealing with his volatile moods, the wedge that ultimately drove Sand and Chopin apart was his involvement with her children. Chopin's relationship with Maurice, whom Sand greatly favored, had never been good, in spite of what seem to have been genuine efforts on Chopin's part to act like a concerned uncle while delicately steering clear of any actions that might have made it seem as though he was trying to take Casimir Dudevant's place. But as Maurice passed through adolescence, his resentment of Chopin grew, and he began to assert himself as the man of the household. Sand's beautiful daughter, Solange, disliked and neglected shamefully by her mother, sought Chopin's protection within the fragile, treacherous web of this peculiar assembled family. Naïve but manipulative, Solange managed to make Sand suspicious that a love had developed between herself and the frail Chopin, whose need for mothering and medical attention far outweighed any desire he may have had for a new lover.

In the summer of 1845, Solange had become engaged to Fernand de Preaux, scion of a solid family that lived near Nohant. The following winter, while in Paris to make arrangements for the wedding, Sand and Solange met Auguste Clésinger, a handsome, heavy-drinking, reasonably talented sculptor, who swept both mother and daughter off their feet. He seduced Solange, who told Sand that she would not marry Preaux; against the advice of friends (but not Chopin, who was in Paris), Sand gave her consent. Solange then seems to have provoked several dreadful family fights, including one brawl during which Clésinger and Sand exchanged blows and the two had to be separated.

Sand threw her daughter and son-in-law out of Nohant. Solange wrote to Chopin, telling him approximately half the story and asking his permission to take the carriage he had left at the house. Sand snapped when she learned of Chopin's polite, concerned response, writing him a furious letter that has not survived. Telling Chopin that he must sever all connections with Solange and Clésinger if their own relationship was to continue, she also apparently unloaded all her pent-up anger in a long and bitter diatribe that left Chopin shocked and hurt. Having finally learned that Solange was pregnant and that Sand had banished her from Nohant, he wrote what seems to have been his last note to his companion of the last nine years:

> This misfortune must be very powerful today if you can forbid your heart to listen to any message of your daughter, at the beginning of her life as a woman, at the very moment when her physical condition calls more than ever for a mother's care. When faced with such grave realities involving your most sacred affections, I must pass over in silence that which concerns me personally. Time will do its work. I shall wait—*still the same as ever.*

This evoked another windy, self-righteous letter from Sand, who chose to

> maintain my right to play the part of the outraged mother...nothing will induce me to allow the authority and dignity of my role to be slighted.... Adieu my friend. May you soon recover from all your ills.... I shall thank God for this queer end to nine years of exclusive friendship. Let me hear now and then how you are. There is no point in ever discussing the other matters.

The relationship was indeed finished. Chopin remained in touch with Solange, who was one of the many family members, friends, and admirers who visited the composer in his final days, but she and her mother never reconciled. Chopin and Sand met once, by chance, in Paris, where they chatted briefly about Solange's baby daughter, shook hands (Sand recalled that Chopin's was cold), and then parted forever.

The breakup with Sand must have accelerated Chopin's decline; his time as a productive composer was coming to an end. Certainly his output dropped significantly from 1847 until his death, although he continued to teach, often lying on a couch, and very occasionally to play for friends. To net some much-needed cash, Chopin played one last semipublic performance in the Salle Pleyel in January 1848 with cellist Franchomme and violinist Jean-Delphin Alard. Opening with what had to be one of the greatest performances ever of a Mozart trio, there were also several solo selections and three of the four movements of the Cello Sonata with Franchomme. In a familiar refrain, one reviewer wrote that Chopin's playing "has no equal in our earthly realm."

Chopin had for several years taught Jane Wilhemina Stirling, a wealthy Scottish amateur who idolized and adored the composer. Stirling stepped into many of Sand's functions as Chopin's caretaker and manager, although his feelings for Stirling never had the depth of those he held for Sand. Stirling also played another crucial role in the composer's last few years: that of benefactor. Always willing to contribute to Chopin's upkeep, anonymously or under the guise of loans, Stirling had the resources to support Chopin when it was becoming increasingly difficult for him to work. Often too ill to teach, and no longer publishing new works, Chopin's income declined at a time when his medical expenses were steadily on the rise. For years Stirling had urged Chopin to tour England, where his works were well known and much admired. With the need to earn money pressing—social and political upheavals turning Paris into a war zone—Chopin finally agreed, arriving in London on April 19, 1848. Stirling had him installed in elegant Mayfair quarters, with three pianos and many other niceties provided, including monogrammed stationery and his favorite cocoa.

Perhaps predictably, Chopin was appalled by the damp chill of the lingering winter and by the fog that covered the city at the time. Stirling, who was a member of the London elite, introduced him to her friends, who soon invited the eminent composer to their homes to play. The Duchess of Sutherland, a confidante of Queen Victoria's, had Chopin, another pianist, and three of the greatest singers of the era to her home at a soiree on May 15, which the Queen attended. Her famously musical consort Prince Albert (who had been an admirer and friend of Mendelssohn's) was sufficiently intrigued by Chopin's playing to get up and stand next to the piano, but the Queen herself only noted in her diary that "several pianists" had performed.

Chopin played several recitals and made a bit of money around the city, but he was also unwell again, spitting blood and suffering from insomnia. As the social season ended, the aristocracy headed for their homes in the country, and Chopin had little choice but to go with Stirling to her properties in Scotland. While enjoying the picturesque landscape and castles, Chopin found himself unhappy with his hosts (both Stirling and her sister Mrs. Erskine, who attempted to convert this nonpracticing Catholic and dandified ultra-aesthete to her own brand of Scottish Calvinism) and felt steadily weaker. "Panting until dinner," Chopin reported in a letter to his friend Albert Grzymala that he sat with the gentlemen, "watching them talk and listening to them drink." As Chopin spoke no English, his hosts politely spoke their rudimentary French, but Chopin was terribly bored. Too weak to climb the stairs, Chopin's manservant had to carry him to his room, where he lay "gasping and dreaming" until morning. Returning to London in the fall, he played at a benefit for Polish relief. He was also examined by one of the royal physicians, who, seeing that nothing could be done in Chopin's case, advised him to return to Paris, where at least his spirits might improve.

In late November 1848, Chopin returned to his apartment in the Square d'Orleans in Paris. Reviving a bit in the milder weather, he was able to eat decently and speak French and Polish with his friends. He took up teaching again on a limited basis but without the energy of old; as a result, his income fell to a trickle. Now completely dependent on charity, he was forced to accept grants from friends, including the Rothschilds, and a huge cash gift from Jane Stirling. He moved in June to the suburb of Chaillot in the hope that its fresh air might help, but there was no mistaking that his decline was irreversible. In addition to coughing blood, Chopin found his limbs beginning to swell as kidney failure set in. Chopin wrote to his sister Ludwika in Warsaw, imploring her to come to Paris, which she did, arriving on August 9th. In a last attempt to find quarters where Chopin might be comfortable, he was moved to a ground floor apartment at 12 Place Vendome, in the heart of the most fashionable district of Paris. With Chopin's assets at low ebb, Stirling and other friends covered the rent.

By early October, Chopin's days were clearly numbered. Friends gathered to bid farewell to the failing man; musicians, including Franchomme, sometimes played from the adjoining room. Sand never came. Perhaps unable to speak, Chopin scribbled a note that read: "If this cough suffocates me, I beg you to have my body opened that I not be buried alive," laying out the full horror of his illness with its constant pressure to breathe. Chopin died in the early morning of Wednesday, October 17, 1849.

Auguste Clésinger was summoned to take casts of Chopin's hands, which are extraordinarily beautiful, and a death mask. That ghastly artifact shows a bloated face, its mouth twisted by the effort to breathe, beneath a bald head. The features become clear as Chopin's only after long comparison with the single famous photograph taken of him around 1846 or 1847. The mask must have shocked his sister Ludwika, who asked Clésinger to do what he could to change it. The sculptor apparently obliged, creating an idealized image of Chopin's handsome features in his prime, with a lock of hair draped artfully across his forehead. His lavish funeral was held on October 30 at the Church of the Madeleine, with all musical, aristocratic, and fashionable Paris in attendance. Its appalling cost was underwritten by Jane Stirling. Chopin's famous Funeral March was played on the organ, as were his mournful Preludes in E minor and B minor; his dear friend Pauline Viardot sang as one of the soloists in Mozart's great Requiem. Chopin was buried in Père-Lachaise Cemetery in Paris, but without his heart, which had been removed when his body was opened after his death, according to his wishes. That object was placed in an urn and sent to the Church of the Holy Cross in Warsaw, where it remains.

Big Ideas in Small Packages
The Etudes and Preludes

Most of Chopin's music is of relatively short duration, with few pieces running longer than twelve minutes. (The only exceptions are the first movements of the two piano concertos.) Brevity is just one aspect of Chopin's compositional technique, and combined with high passion, musical density, and richness of texture, it gives his music a sound that is instantly identifiable. For Chopin, short forms are not miniatures, but highly compressed genres in which one or two ideas can be set forth in their individual character—whether lyrical, stormy, exotic, or grotesque—and then explored in ways that are often highly unconventional but absolutely complete. Chopin ends when he has had his say, never flogging his ideas in wearisome repetition. Nowhere is his mastery of short forms clearer than in the etudes and the preludes.

Chopin published twenty-seven *etudes,* or studies. Everyone who has studied the piano is familiar with the etude, generally from playing those written by Cramer and Czerny. Recognizing technical problems that stem from the differences in strength of the fingers (the fourth being the weakest, followed by the fifth), keyboard players and teachers as far back as Bach have devised short works that follow repetitive patterns to help students achieve greater finger independence and strength. The vast bulk of these etudes are mechanical pieces with no pretension to art that serve as technical building blocks for beginners and intermediate students. Chopin's etudes also deal with mechanical difficulties, but on a heroic scale, all requiring the skills of a virtuoso pianist. And even some of the greatest pianists have been intimidated by the finger-twisting complexity of these short masterpieces:

Arthur Rubinstein, perhaps the greatest all-around Chopin player of the twentieth century, never recorded them, as he did the rest of the master's oeuvre two or three times over in the course of his long career, although he did play some in recital. Even the supervirtuoso Vladimir Horowitz, who played many of the etudes brilliantly, is quoted as saying that the one in C major, op. 10, no. 1, did not fit his hand, and the A minor, op. 25, no. 11, was simply too tiring.

Chopin's etudes are the greatest instructional compositions after those of Bach to combine technical difficulty with artistry at the highest level. In the etudes, Chopin addresses a variety of technical problems with large-scale musical ideas and gestures, fitting them into tight forms that he devised individually for each piece. Unlike most studies, there is no formula that all follow. Their rich figuration and the triumph of the pianist over their obvious difficulties add to the scope of each etude, although most take only between two and three minutes to play. (The shortest occupies just over a minute and the longest about six minutes.) While many flaunt their difficulties in flashy sprays of notes at breakneck speeds, several are slow studies in touch and expression, including the E major Etude, op. 10, no. 3, which opens with one of Chopin's most famous melodies; and the profound Etude in C-sharp minor, op. 25, no. 7. This, the longest and slowest etude, is a duet in which the left hand spins out an endless melody of a rich, cellolike character, while the right hand covers a plaintive tune of the sort heard in Italian opera. The pianist and musicologist Charles Rosen has pointed out the similarity of this magnificent takeoff of an operatic scene with the real one for soprano and cello that opens act 2 of *Norma,* by Chopin's friend Bellini.

The first set of etudes, composed between 1830 and '32 and published in 1833 as Chopin's op. 10, opens with a heaven-scaling piece, in which the right hand must range swiftly over vast spans of the keyboard while the left plays a long, bell-like melody. The right hand figurations are called *arpeggios,* referring to the harp (from the Italian *arpa*). This musical term describes chords in which the notes are struck in quick succession rather that all at once; arpeggios are the technical subject of several of the etudes. What is remarkable about this first etude is the heroic voice in which it speaks, despite a playing time of about two minutes; this is the result of its grand melody, wide harmonic range, and the breadth of the arpeggios as they roam insolently over the keyboard.

The second Etude in A minor is a notoriously awkward and difficult study for the third, fourth, and fifth fingers of the right hand, which Chopin forces the player to use repeatedly, but is comically dainty in effect. No. 3, in E major, is a famous study in touch and singing tone, as is no. 6, in E-flat minor. In the fourth piece, in C-sharp minor, the fingers of both hands pass around a quick, fiery melody. Technical problems that inspire the remainder of the op. 10 Etudes include execution of rapid accompaniments, with melodies in the left hand, as in nos. 5, 7, and 8; or in the right, as in no. 12, the so-called Revolutionary Etude. In all of these, Chopin employs large-scale musical ideas to make the pieces sound full, complete, and satisfying.

The two etudes on the enclosed CD are from the second set of twelve, published in 1837 as op. 25. The Etude in A-flat major, op. 25, no. 1, that opens this series is a study in arpeggios, in keyboard color by use of the pedals, and in tying together the notes of a long melody—the musical term for which is *legato,* or "tied." This is antithetical to the nature of the piano, a percussion instrument, but the achievement of legato was one of Chopin's constant goals. He used unconventional notation when writing this piece, marking the melody in a way to make it stand out from the many notes of the accompaniment, which are in small type. In any case, the etude displays Chopin's trademark piano sound in all its exquisite richness.

The work, which takes up track 1 on the CD, opens with the melody—calm and even, but rich in emotion—in the right hand, floating above an elaborate, hazy, mellow accompaniment. The tune is beautiful and easily memorized. Now (0:11) notes played by the left hand—the deeper tones—emerge, not part of the main melody but relevant to it, pushing it and entwining with it. The right-hand melody rises and falls in a huge arc, before finally ending at 0:20. The tune, like many of Chopin's, has a singable quality; here it seems to pause as a singer might for a breath before beginning again.

But after commencing its repeat in the same way it opened, the melody takes a new but equally memorable direction, hovering on a current of different accompanying notes (0:35). At 0:42 the melody takes a fervent new turn, without ever altering its even pulse. Here Chopin changes the harmony of the accompaniment to make the melody sound as though it is searching passionately for some new level; at 1:05 it starts its final reach toward a climactic high note, which is finally achieved at 1:30, with the noble melody pressing ahead in the same even rhythm. It now begins a long and graceful descent, surging upward for one last exquisite high note at 1:46. At 2:02 a series of airy arpeggios sweep up and down the keyboard; their constant hovering motion continues almost to the very end. This magical piece finally comes to rest with a sweet trill in the left hand followed by a quiet, rolled chord. While devising a technical study in which the pianist must sustain a melody over an exceptionally complex accompaniment, Chopin created a vision of rapturous lyricism and unearthly beauty.

The harplike quality of the accompaniment and the airiness of its texture caused a nineteenth-century critic to nickname this etude the "Aeolian Harp," after the mythical instrument of the wind-god Aeolus. Chopin himself detested all impressionistic nicknames and stories fabricated to describe and explain his works, but it isn't too hard to see how this one was dreamed up, even if the main melody has an ardent quality rarely associated with music for the harp. While the beauties of the A-flat Etude are readily apparent, its greatness as music is a more complex matter. The combined perfection of all the elements that go into the piece—starting with the tune itself and continuing with the brilliantly polished, idiomatic keyboard writing that forms Chopin's stylistic signature and makes his music so distinctive—are the most obvious aspects of its quality. No composer wrote music that sounds better conceived for the piano. Chopin's extraordinary restraint and taste are another key. Rather than risk overstatement by dragging out his ideas, no matter how lovely, he presents them in short form, leaving listeners panting for more instead of wishing the work ended even a moment sooner. Yet, as with many of his two-minute masterpieces, the etude feels spacious: there is no sense that it is a miniature or that the form cramps the musical concept.

There is another crucial element of the etude's power to move the listener in Chopin's use of harmony, without which the melody might not sound quite so beautiful. Harmony deals with the relationships between individual notes—how they sound together—and between keys, a key being the tonal "home base" for a musical composition. Classical compositions generally begin and end in their home key, but as all great composers, including Haydn, Mozart, Beethoven, Schubert, Brahms, Verdi, Wagner—and Chopin—realized, music that moves predictably or stays too long in any key quickly becomes dull. These composers move fearlessly among different keys, giving their music a freshness, openness, and tension that stems from the free contrast, and even conflict, of keys, and the sense of a satisfying return to the tonal home base after a prolonged harmonic journey. The chills one feels when a composer restates a melody in a way that sounds different and powerful usually means that the composer has changed the harmony to emphasize the theme in a different way, showing it in another light, as Chopin does in the A-flat major Etude, where he employs the harmony of the undulating accompaniment to push the melody in different directions.

The second etude on the CD (track 2), the brilliant but quirky E minor, op. 25, no. 5, sounds utterly different from its companion piece. Where the A-flat Etude is a single seamless melody embedded in rich and mellow harmony, the E minor consists of a short, jumpy theme over a biting accompaniment that is unusually dissonant for a composition from the mid-1830s. In contrast to the unbroken flow of op. 25, no. 1, this work is in three distinct parts with a strange, vehement closing section. Chopin's suggestions for the speed and character of the piece are *vivace* (lively) and *scherzando* (playful), suggesting that the etude ought not to sound too serious, but there's no getting away from its eccentricity, which is reminiscent of Beethoven in one of his frisky moods.

The opening sets the tone of the piece, with the melody—stated in detached notes in a manic bouncing rhythm—accompanied by an acrid harmony that is strong and unusual. Interestingly, the dissonance becomes less jarring, taking on a more decorative quality as the ear gets used to its sound over the course of the etude. On its second appearance (0:09), the melody, still leaping erratically in the right hand, comes across as even more awkward as the left-hand accompaniment mimics the jerky rhythm of the right. At 0:16 a long note is struck in the middle of the keyboard, with jumpy proceedings continuing all around, and then repeated nine times. It is the first of several obsessively repeated notes and chords that form another aspect of the musical substance of this etude, in which islands of stability show up in the midst of apparent disorder.

A flurry of notes in the right hand (0:25) compresses the theme into a form that is barely recognizable. But the theme returns at 0:29, presented in a different rhythmic guise in the right hand but retaining the original, bouncing broken chords in the left; another restatement at 0:37 presents the material in another more even but still nervous rhythm. At 0:43 three bouncing notes—separated by long pauses, with the hands far apart on the keys—introduce the middle section (0:53), marked *piu lento* (more slowly). This episode contrasts strikingly with the opening. Chopin changes the key signature to E major, the tonal opposite of E minor, and broadens the melody, giving it to the left hand to play in long, legato notes, with the right providing a lush, sweeping accompaniment. The tune passes (1:14) from the middle of the keyboard into the booming bass notes, in a figuration that will reappear briefly just before the end. It is repeated at 1:43 against a more animated right-hand accompaniment, all of which fade gradually away, permitting the return of the opening section.

The tune and its accompaniment go through a few brief new permutations; at 2:42 a long note appears in the middle of it all, to be repeated eight times. The three bouncing notes that marked the end of the first section reappear (2:53), the second and third of them interspersed by three notes in the bass (2:57) in a final, fragmentary appearance of the theme in its middle-section guise. At 3:05 an E major chord is hammered emphatically eight times, bursting into a long trill before this remarkable work ends in a rainbow of notes arching up the keyboard.

This etude, unlike the ecstatic A-flat, is an intellectual puzzle in which Chopin playfully challenges listeners to acclimate themselves to a highly dissonant idiom, follow him as he toys with the E minor and E major tonalities, and track an erratic theme through fast-moving rhythmic and tonal incarnations. The pianist's job is to make the theme intelligible in each of its manifestations, dealing all the while with the work's formidable technical demands.

The other high points of the op. 25 set include no. 2 in F minor, a difficult and delicate study in contrasting rhythms, and the bouncy no. 3 in F major, for which the performer uses the same fingering in each of the 204 repetitions of the short phrase from which the work is built. No. 4 in A minor is a fantastically beautiful and poetic study in contrasting touches, in which most notes are played quickly while others must be held down—a difficult feat. The sixth Etude in G-sharp minor is also infamously challenging, with the player having to negotiate multiple notes in a close, uncomfortable hand position.

All of the three final works in the opus are large-scale and of immense power: no. 10 in B minor is a thunderous study in octaves with a ripely melodic central episode, and no. 11 is the merciless A minor (popularly nicknamed "Winter Wind") that intimidated even Horowitz. In no. 12 in C minor, vast arpeggios sweep up and down the keyboard while the left hand tolls the melody in the bass. This mighty variant of the Etude in C major, op. 10, no. 1, was once nicknamed "The Ocean"; as with the "Aeolian Harp," the epithet may be unnecessary, but as an impression it is not completely off the mark. The three etudes without opus number called the *Trois Nouvelles Études* are of prevailingly lyrical character and fully equal in stature to the pieces on op. 10 and 25, with no. 2 in A-flat being hauntingly beautiful.

Nowhere is Chopin's ability to compress his ideas demonstrated more vividly than in his preludes. Most take less than two minutes to play, but all are powerfully, even shockingly, expressive. In these short works, Chopin sets out in unforgettable clarity one musical idea or two at most, some of which are his most striking and strange. Along with the mazurkas, these contain Chopin's boldest, bravest, most forward-looking music.

The preludes are contained in a set of twenty-four, published in 1839 as Chopin's op. 28. There is also a single, extended, and beautiful Prelude in C-sharp minor, op. 45, from 1841 that is awesomely prescient of Brahms, and a lonely but lovely Prelude in A-flat major, composed in

1834 but not published until 1918. Chopin composed op. 28 with Bach on his mind: each of the pieces is in one of the twenty-four major and minor keys, following the model of the baroque master's two monumental sets of preludes and fugues that make up books 1 and 2 of *The Well-Tempered Clavier.*

Chopin's interest in the different tonal color of each key is a crucial element in his conception of the works individually and of the group as a whole. Some of the preludes in major keys are anything but bright and cheerful—such as the first in C major, which is emotional and clouded with dissonance—while the E major is weird and grandiose, and the A-flat major is all in twilight tones. The D-flat major, saddled with the unfortunate nickname "Raindrop," by far the longest of the pieces, is in mood and structure much like a nocturne, with a spectral middle section. Not all the preludes in minor keys are "sad." The one in C-sharp minor flashes and sparkles, and the B-flat minor is fierce, fiery, and spirited.

It is now nearly impossible to hear the op. 28 Preludes performed live other than as a complete forty-minute set, usually taking up the second half of a recital program. One reason is the need by pianists to be taken seriously as interpretive artists, capable of tying the twenty-four into a cohesive cycle; another is to insure that Chopin is seen as a large-scale, long-range musical thinker, in accordance with today's earnest aesthetic standards—help he doesn't need, by the way. Without question, the set of twenty-four forms a satisfying emotional arc, opening with the surging, prefatory piece in C major; moving through contrasting keys to a mid-point at the big D-flat Prelude; and ultimately reaching the desolate fury of the D minor Prelude, which ends the series with three shattering hammer blows. But it was not Chopin's intention or his own custom to perform the preludes as a complete set. He generally played three or four at a sitting or one alone as a lead-in to a larger work, often in a complementary key. For example, at one performance he appears to have played the swirling F-sharp minor Prelude (track 4 on the included CD) as an introduction to the Impromptu no. 2 in F-sharp major.

A prelude by definition precedes another work, often one that is weightier or longer, and it was customary in the nineteenth and early twentieth centuries for pianists in recital to play brief preludes, consisting of a few soft chords or a bit of passagework, before launching into a programmed piece. But unlike Chopin's intense and elaborate preludes, these were generally improvised throwaways of negligible musical substance. Like those of Bach, whose preludes in *The Well-Tempered Clavier* occasionally dwarf the fugues that follow, Chopin's preludes lack nothing in power and gravity compared with any of his other music. Indeed, they are as a group perhaps his most dense and expressive compositions. Performance practices have simply changed, with the pendulum having swung to playing the op. 28 Preludes complete. But Chopin did not conceive them to be performed in one sitting.

Track 3 of the CD is the Prelude in E minor, the fourth of the set of twenty-four. Chopin composed this well-known work in Majorca, during his disastrous visit with George Sand and her children in the autumn and winter of 1838–39. According to many accounts, Chopin performed it often himself; it was played at his funeral. The work opens with a three-note sequence that struggles weakly upward in the right hand, supported by soft, sad chords in the left. For the entire first half of the piece, the right-hand melody moves in the narrowest range: up a note, then down, then up again, then down again. Throughout, the left-hand chords exert a subtle downward pull, changing gently but always descending a note here and a note there.

The melody makes a hopeless attempt at 0:37 to break out of the pattern of long notes in a narrow range, in which it utterly fails, the original drooping melody returning at 0:41 over wavering chords in the left hand. At 0:51, the right-hand melody breaks out into an eloquent but mournful phrase as the left hand pauses as though exhausted. The long, slow melody starts again at 0:57, but now the left hand sinks more rapidly. At 1:12 the melody struggles to its biggest climax in an outburst that has, like many of Chopin's melodic phrases, a passionate quality strongly reminiscent of the Italian opera he adored, but this one is short and restricted in range, running out of breath by 1:28. Again at 1:30, the drooping melody begins, pulled down once more by pulsing chords in the left hand, which now move inexorably downward, striking a hollow shift in harmony at 1:41. The melody and its accompaniment die at 1:56; there is a long, terrible pause, followed by three long, sepulchral chords that bring this extraordinary expression of despair to an end. As noted, Chopin hated all attempts to attach stories to his pieces, but it's impossible not to hear the terror and hopelessness of the composer, desperately ill and isolated in his damp room in Majorca, in this fearful music.

Chopin's impact on composers who followed was enormous. One of the greatest of those he influenced was Richard Wagner, the titan of late romantic German opera, who seems to have studied Chopin's music productively. In all likelihood, Wagner heard it played by Franz Liszt, Chopin's one-time friend and colleague and also Wagner's friend, confidant, and father-in-law; Chopin's daring, advanced ideas were far from lost on the alert Wagner.

On the surface, the music of Wagner and Chopin seem quite different: the pithy Pole wrote scarcely anything as long as twenty-five minutes, whereas Wagner's epic music dramas generally take about five hours to perform. What Wagner learned from Chopin was about harmony, both composers being among the boldest harmonists in the history of classical music, and tone painting, the art of using instruments to create images in sound. Wagner's tone painting provided the audiences of his operas with vivid aural images that might describe a character, such as a forest bird; or an event, such as a storm. Chopin's tone painting is more often abstract but no less striking; obviously, Wagner used a big orchestra, while Chopin achieved his effects on the piano. Chopin's Prelude in F-sharp minor, op. 28, no. 8 (track 4 on the CD), composed in 1838 or '39, is a remarkable anticipation in tone and character of an orchestral interlude from one of Wagner's mature operas (the earliest of which is *Das Rhiengold* of 1853–54) and a good example of Chopin's influence on another major composer.

The piece opens in a swirling storm of notes, in which an agitated melody of tightly limited range is wrapped. Neither the thick texture of the piano sound nor the stormy nature of the music will change over the course of the work. At 0:12 the theme, having been played through once, is repeated, now sounding more restless and unsettled. Every repetition of the theme is a little different from the one it follows—one soft, another loud—but the effect is of a relentless, ever-intensifying turbulence. At 0:30 the theme takes on a beseeching note; at 0:55 the piece reaches a climax, marked by Chopin to be played *molto agitato*;

at 1:06 the melody is pushed to its highest pitch, after which (1:20) it begins to subside, without providing any sense of emotional relief. A tiny change in the harmony at 1:29 moderates the color of this tempest to a slightly lighter shade of gray, but it darkens once more (1:36). Four brusque chords (1:41) bring this agitated tone painting to an uneasy end.

The F-sharp minor Prelude is one of the most difficult of the op. 28 set to play, resembling an etude, like a number of its companion pieces. Texturally the work is very much like the ecstatic A-flat major Etude, op. 25, no. 1, that opens the CD, with its melody buried in a blizzard of accompanying notes, but the tone and mood of the two works could hardly be more different. It is easy to imagine a Wagnerian orchestration of this piece, with the theme taken by brass and the billowing notes of the accompaniment in the strings.

If the F-sharp minor Prelude can be thought of as orchestral in texture, the F major, op. 28, no. 23 (track 5), is piano writing at its purest. In this joyous little work, Chopin plays with a simple-sounding arpeggiated melody over a delicious left-hand accompaniment. The magical piece is over barely before we realize, opening with a rolled chord in the left hand, accompanied by an evenly rippling tune that is made of the lightest figuration in the right. Almost immediately (0:03), the left hand comes in with a trill in the bass, followed by a marvelous rocking figure (0:05) that spins its way importantly through the course of the work. Listen at 0:15 for a slightly off-sounding note at the tail end of the rocking figure: it adds flash of hazy color and will return in telling fashion twice more. Again at 0:24 we hear another note, slightly clashing, adding just a bit of richness to the pure F-major harmony. The dissonance comes back one last time at 0:44, making the work spin off ecstatically, as if into thin air, in the last breathless moment before this sequence of exquisite shivers comes to an end.

The Prelude in A minor, op. 28, no. 2 (track 6), is a leading candidate for Chopin's strangest piece. Radically modern and mysterious in message, these two minutes of music look a century ahead to the expressionist gems of Anton von Webern. The A minor Prelude opens in the left hand with a repeated figure in the sourest harmony, making the music, which is actually rhythmically steady, sound as though it limps. At 0:08 the right hand chimes in with a theme of repeated notes that can barely be called a melody, ending (0:24) in a rhythm reminiscent of a funeral march. The left hand continues its steady course, the harmony changing but remaining ugly. At 0:34 the right-hand statement is repeated at a higher pitch, with the left hand changing color but not its inward and impenetrable affect. The tune begins again (1:03) in long-held notes, but at 1:18 the left hand stops, allowing the right hand to complete its declaration. From 1:30 to 1:36, the left hand comes in for one last, brief comment; the right hand finishes the phrase with the marchlike figure (1:39), and a handful of chords (1:49) end this most inhospitable of the preludes. Chopin's emotions must have been polar when he wrote it: nothing could be bleaker than the grinding harmonies that grip the piece from start to finish, and this could be the most cramped and unvocal tune written by this great melodist. Perhaps most striking is the way the work's back seems always to be turned to the listener. It must have baffled Chopin's contemporaries, because it remains tough going today.

The preludes show Chopin at his most daring and musically advanced. Even his great supporter Robert Schumann found them difficult, describing them tellingly as "sketches, beginnings of etudes . . . ruins, individual eagle pinions, all disorder and wild confusion." The preludes were simply too strange, dense, and forward-looking, even for a sympathetic critic and composer of genius like Schumann. The F-sharp minor Prelude may remind listeners of Wagner in tone, but its compression could hardly be further in scale from that master's mammoth works, which effectively brought the romantic movement in music to a point past which it could not continue. Later composers looked to the example of Chopin, not Wagner, for keys to music's direction: the effect of the etudes and preludes on his followers was direct and potent.

The Russians Scriabin and Rachmaninoff added dozens of etudes and preludes to the piano repertory for the piano, but Chopin's truest heir has to be Claude Debussy, whose own magnificent musical vision—expressed in twenty-four preludes, twelve etudes, and other piano works—pick up where Chopin left off, boldly shaping the music of the twentieth century.

The Music for Piano and Orchestra

hopin's two piano concertos and the handful of other works for piano and orchestra are all products of his early years as a composer, with the Concerto no. 1, op. 11, from 1830 being the latest. (The slightly later, fully mature *Andante spianato* and *Grande polonaise brillante,* op. 22, has an orchestral part so insignificant that the paired works are rarely played as anything but a solo). In these pieces, the young Chopin made his obeisance to the musical culture of the day, in which a pianist was expected to compose works for piano and orchestra in a style suited to display his particular strengths as a player—in Chopin's case, his delicacy of touch and peerless ability to execute ornamental runs. They are as a group Chopin's least original works and also those most maligned by musical critics, but they contain much material of interest, charm, and real beauty. The two concertos remain popular and are enormously effective when well played. The other works with orchestra, while not masterpieces, have been unjustly neglected; they surely merit occasional performances by pianists in sympathy with their elegant style.

The concertos were composed and published in reverse order, with no. 2 in F minor written in 1829 but revised before publication in 1836; the E minor Concerto was composed in 1830 and printed in 1833. The F minor work is the more artful, with an opening theme that slides in gracefully as opposed to the slightly pompous statement that begins the E minor Concerto, but the musical material of these nearly contemporaneous works is otherwise quite similar. Over the years, critics have complained chiefly about Chopin's unadventurous harmony and orchestration in the concertos. Indeed, the harmony in both works is surprisingly static for this normally bold explorer, with very little in the way of his typical wanderings. With one or two small exceptions, all six movements stay close—*too* close—to their home keys and nearest relatives, but it should be remembered that they were written just before Chopin began to kick hard against the restraints of classical harmony in his first sets of mazurkas (opp. 6 and 7) and nocturnes (op. 9) composed mostly between 1830 and 1832.

To ears accustomed to the lush and massive orchestral accompaniments in the concertos of Brahms, Tchaikovsky, and Ravel, Chopin's will surely sound spare, if not impoverished. But they are entirely comparable to the orchestral writing of the opera composer Vincenzo Bellini, his friend and colleague, whose scores are fine boned and conservative but suited to their purpose, and which, like Chopin's, have resisted subsequent tampering in the name of improvement. When Georges Bizet, the composer of *Carmen,* was asked to rescore Bellini's *Norma,* he refused, commenting: "For these melodies the appropriate accompaniment is that given to them by Bellini." What Bizet meant was that Bellini's vast, sublime vocal melodies needed nothing more in the way of orchestral background than what their composer had provided.

Chopin's piano in the concertos is not unlike a Bellini singer, usually carrying Italianate vocal-styled themes fused to his inimitable keyboard writing. As with Bellini, rescoring Chopin's accompaniment can only throw off the delicate balance of solo and orchestral parts. While breaking no new ground, Chopin's orchestration in the concertos is often pleasing and effective. There are some lovely moments for winds, particularly the clarinets and bassoons, in both; a charming horn call marks the closing section of the F minor Concerto; and there is an amusing moment in the finale of the E minor Concerto where the violin players are asked to tap their strings with the wood of their bows. When the full orchestra plays during that movement, it is with a bright, trumpet-dominated sound that is almost baroque.

Listeners who expect Chopin to plumb Mozartian depths in his concertos are bound for disappointment: they are works composed without reference to and almost surely without knowledge of those pinnacles of the concerto literature. Nor was Chopin likely to have heard Beethoven's, which were not played in the Warsaw of his youth. Chopin's concertos are modeled on the works of such lesser composer-pianists as Kalkbrenner, Ries, and Hummel, now remembered mostly in history books, while Chopin's are very much part of the active repertory. Whatever their weaknesses, these works abound in felicities that make them worthwhile. The emotions they express may be more affected than real, masks the composer picks up and drops as the needs of the concerto form dictate. But in both slow movements, Chopin is not far from his best— offering music that is inimitably beautiful and touching, at moments nearly profound—and both finales are tightly crafted and pleasing to listen to.

The F minor Concerto, op. 21, opens with a musical question and answer that is a staple of the concerto form. The strings begin with a soft descending phrase that is the query, followed immediately by a brusque reply by the full orchestra. A new melodic phrase begins quietly but soon grows agitated, leading to a big orchestral outburst. After this calms down, the winds state a lyrical second theme, which eventually builds to an explosion in the orchestra. Soon the piano enters with a powerful run, introducing condensed, heavily ornamented versions of the opening themes. One of the piano's key roles throughout is to decorate these with fantastic embellishments, much as would soon be heard in the nocturnes, where the same kind of operatic melodies are elaborated with sprays of notes that are often wild but always relevant.

After all the themes have been restated by the piano, in dialogue with the strings and horns, the soloist takes up a series of runs that sweep up and down the keyboard with choreographic grace. The piano then presents the second, lyrical theme—alone and, again, heavily ornamented. The orchestra gradually joins in, but the piano dominates the proceedings throughout this middle of the movement, where the various melodies are broken up, combined, and elaborated with taste, élan, and skill, if not Beethovenian strength. Toward the end, the piano engages the various wind instruments in mellow colloquy, but ultimately the orchestra wins out with a forceful statement.

For Chopin, the tempo marking *larghetto,* (the diminutive of *largo,* or broad) which he employs for the slow movements of both concertos, denotes music that is songful, flowing, and lavishly embellished. Thus, the second movement of the F minor Concerto opens with a long melody ending in a heart-easing phrase that represents the deepest emotion evoked in the concertos. Although the elaborations that follow may be predictable, they are gorgeous nonetheless. But then Chopin takes a bold step: halfway through the movement, introduced by powerful runs for the soloist, the strings play a series of trembling figures to accompany the keyboard as it chants a series of phrases, in which, as Charles Rosen points out, Chopin pays direct homage to Italian opera. Here he imitates a scene in which two characters, both portrayed by the piano, can be heard in passionate dialogue. The opening melody returns in all its glory to end this tender and magnificent tribute to Italian opera, one of Chopin's constant inspirations, which here, as always, he adapted completely to the range, resources, and sonority of the piano.

The last movement is an elegant essay in dance rhythms that drifts from mazurka to waltz and back again several times. The texture of the writing for the piano is entirely lighter and more open than in the first two movements, with a consequent relaxation of the dramatic tensions of the opening movement and the lyric intensity of the larghetto. Midway through there is some graceful discourse between the horns and piano, before the horn calls, based on a mazurka-like theme earlier in the movement, signal a change of key and an acceleration into a cheerful scramble for the finish that engages the pianist in more overtly virtuosic work.

The E minor Concerto, op. 11, opens with a blustery statement that lacks Chopin's usual subtlety. It does, however, enfold a sorrowful variant of the main theme over a throbbing accompaniment that is used effectively later on, and a lyrical second theme in E major. The piano enters with the first theme (sounding better on the solo instrument than it does in the full orchestra) and then takes up the sorrowful portion in a richly decorated version. As in the F minor Concerto, fast-moving passagework rounds out the thematic group. Piano and orchestra debate; as is often the case in a concerto, the piano, representing the individual, loses out to the greater numbers of the orchestra. The first movement of this work has many moments of great beauty and may be structured a bit more tightly than its opposite number in op. 21, but the expressive qualities of the latter make it undeniably more appealing.

With the second and third movements of the E minor Concerto, however, Chopin returns to form. The second movement, which Chopin entitles Romanze, is an exquisite nocturne for piano and orchestra, in which the soloist elaborates on a shapely theme to which a long, drooping closing phrase, much like those heard in many of the nocturnes, is appended. Chopin makes no dramatic gestures in this slow movement, as he did in the middle section of the F minor Concerto's, but there is a powerful shift of harmony at the movement's climax, and throughout, the silvery cool piano writing revels in the sound and expressive capabilities of the instrument. The finale of the E minor Concerto is another movement based on Polish dance, this one a brisk but delicate *krakowiak,* a two-step not unlike a polka. Throughout the movement, the piano drapes the main theme with decorations that are exquisite and amusing, and at last there is a brief but startling drop from E major to a dreamy-sounding E-flat major, hinting at the more daring harmonic experiments Chopin would soon undertake.

The three other works for piano with orchestra are rarely heard but readily merit occasional performance. The Variations on *Là ci darem la mano* from Mozart's *Don Giovanni,* op. 2, is conceived on a surprisingly large scale for a seventeen-year-old, even if it does nothing more than decorate Mozart's tune and display the pianist's technique. In a display of his budding interest in his national music, Chopin writes one variation as a polonaise. The work dazzled audiences and critics of its day. The Fantasy on Polish Airs, op. 13, based on several folk songs and dances, is a lovely trifle, while the Krakowiak Concert Rondo, op. 14, written by Chopin for his 1829 Vienna debut, is a more substantial piece with an infectious, rhythmic bounce.

Dance Idealized
The Waltzes

The rhythms of dance form the bedrock of music. All composers have employed dance in their works. Its pulse makes up the backbone of a staggeringly high proportion of the repertory, from the music of Claudio Monteverdi (1567–1643), which is saturated with dance, through the twentieth century. Dance animates most of Bach's music: in addition to the vast array of sarabandes, allemandes, loures, minuets, gavottes, sicilianos, passepieds, courantes, gigues, bourées—and even a handful of polonaises—in his instrumental sonatas and suites, there are countless other movements throughout his work that are in dance form and rhythm, although not accorded their titles as dances.

Handel set many of the arias in his operas and oratorios to dance forms, particularly favoring the gavotte and minuet. Every string quartet and symphony by Haydn and almost all of Mozart's and Beethoven's early compositions in these forms contain minuets; these giants, like Bach and Handel, used dance rhythm for many other pieces as well. One of Beethoven's greatest works for piano, the Diabelli Variations, op. 120, consists of thirty-three mind-bending reconfigurations of a shockingly trivial waltz by the Viennese publisher and composer Anton Diabelli. Among Chopin's contemporaries, Schumann was a marvelous writer of waltzes, notably in the *Davidsbundlertänze,* op. 6, and *Caranval,* op. 9; his *Papillons,* op. 2, is a suite of dances in the style of Schubert, but with Schumann's characteristic blend of dreamy and passionate emotion.

Chopin's great followers Debussy and Ravel were both masters of dance form. Debussy was fascinated by the sharp rhythms of Spanish dance and the forms of his musical ancestors of the French baroque.

Ravel's *Valses Nobles et Sentimentales* is a loving look back on the waltz suites of Schubert; the orchestral tone poem *La valse* casts an ironic eye on the Viennese version of the dance.

The music written by great composers in dance forms are generally far from their rough origins in popular dance. Certainly Chopin's fourteen canonic waltzes—symphonic in dimension, regal in tone, and rich in experimental content—are a long way from anything called a waltz that came before or after. Like Bach's dance pieces, Chopin's waltzes (like his mazurkas and polonaises) are not ballroom dances but rather meditations on the dance and choreographic dramas. No composer surpassed Chopin in the form, where perhaps his only equal is Johann Strauss, the Viennese master of big orchestral waltzes. In Chopin's waltzes, as in Bach's mighty dance movements, form, rhythm and melody are distilled into profound organisms too musically and emotionally complex for movement on a ballroom floor. Chopin took a coarse and common dance (the German verb *walzen* means "to wallow," a censorious description of the dancers' movements) that was performed in beer gardens and homes, abstracting, refining, and idealizing it in the process.

Schubert composed dozens of lovely, soulful waltzes and *ländlers,* another Austrian dance in the same family, but these are short and formally—if not emotionally—simple, usually consisting of two parts, both repeated, the melodies played more softly and delicately the second time around. They were written in the 1810s and '20s, when the waltz, one of the first dances to be performed by couples holding each other rather than men and women in groups, was passing from its status as a dangerous favorite of the lower classes and the daring young to acceptance in wider and higher social circles. Schubert's waltzes, like Chopin's, are intended for listening—for thoughtful consideration of their lyricism and countless subtleties—rather than dancing. A pupil of Chopin's reported that the composer knew and taught many of Schubert's dances.

Another important influence on Chopin as a writer of waltzes was Carl Maria von Weber, the fine early-romantic composer, whose *Invitation to the Dance* of 1819 adds to the waltz suite of Schubert a dramatic *mise en scène,* in which the waltzes are framed by recitative-like passages that portray the conversation of two dancers in the ballroom. Once immensely popular, Weber's piece is now heard most often as a light classical radio staple in an orchestral version that seems less effective than the original piano score. In the imaginative passage that opens the work, the left hand takes the part of the gentleman, making polite (but wordless) conversation, to which the right hand, depicting the lady, replies with coquettish grace. The man then invites the woman to dance; she accepts, they take to the floor, and the dances begin. In turn sweeping, tender, and fiery, the waltzes come and go in a lively interplay; after they end, the left hand thanks the right, which expresses demure pleasure as the piece fades to an artful ending.

These "speaking" passages are also prescient of a number of pages in Chopin, including those in the second movement of the F minor Concerto, and the Etude in C-sharp minor, op. 25, no. 7, in which the piano eloquently imitates human speech and song. Chopin knew Weber's piece well; there are accounts of his playing it. Chopin seems to have learned from *Invitation to the Dance* how to give his own waltzes a dramatic framework that is not as concrete as Weber's but is palpable nonetheless, particularly in the waltzes that begin with calls that summon the dancers to the floor.

Chopin's first published waltz, the E-flat major, op. 18, subtitled *Grande valse brillante,* opens with such a call, reminiscent of a trumpet (the piece is sometimes nicknamed the "Trumpet Waltz"), and is closer in form and spirit to the works of Schubert and Weber than any of Chopin's waltzes. It is actually a medley of six thematically related dances, some of contrasting character, all tied together with the introductory flourish and an elaborate and remarkable closing section. Of particular interest is the apparent variety of the melodies, which Chopin compresses skillfully at the end in a way that shows how closely they are actually related. That *coda* (closing section) begins boldly with the left hand stating the unaccompanied waltz rhythm. While it may sound a bit impersonal in comparison with the highly charged emotions of some of the later waltzes, the perpetual popularity of this dance is easily explained by its tunefulness and masterful construction.

The three waltzes that comprise Chopin's op. 34 are varied in content, and show marked advances in compositional technique and expressive range over op. 18. The first in the set, in A-flat major, opens like its predecessor with a call summoning the imaginary dancers to the floor, but here the call is far more subtle and graceful than the straightforward rhythmic rapping that begins the E-flat Waltz. It is, moreover, reinterpreted by the second of the four dances that make up the piece. The long coda, which is just as elaborate as its predecessor's and more dramatically apt, opens with a fiery statement that moves into some fast passagework over a left-hand accompaniment that jumps the rails of the standard "oom-pah-pah" waltz beat, suggesting the feverish excitement of a ballroom scene.

The third Waltz of op. 34, in F major, also starts with a muster to the dance floor, this time a series of chords in a strong rhythm. These are followed by a swirl of notes suggesting a string orchestra or perhaps what a listener might hear when approaching the ballroom, before the left hand catches up with the rhythm, sometimes losing it in an amusing scramble between the two hands that is actually well under control. There is a wistful harmonic shift in the middle section that carries the third theme to a place far from the dance floor.

The second Waltz of op. 34, in A minor, stands apart from its companion works and from all the other waltzes. In this slow waltz, there is again no illusion of actual dancing but rather an exploration of a mood, as the left hand takes up the inward-looking theme in tones reminiscent of the cello while the right renders the waltz beat with a limp. The right hand then decorates the second part of the theme with simple but exquisite passagework. Even the contrasting theme in A major is somber, and is soon repeated in A minor. Some beautiful cellolike figures in the left hand accompany a series of gorgeous chords in the right, leading to the final statement of the introverted opening melody. This tone poem in miniature is marked by a Slavic gloom of the darkest hue, bringing it much closer in spirit to the more meditative mazurkas—such as op. 17, no. 4, in the same key—and shows a clear influence on Tchaikovsky and Sibelius.

The Waltz in A-flat, op. 42, one of the greatest of the series, is a masterpiece of Chopin's maturity. This astonishing work has a cinematic sweep, moving from the most inspired introductory passage of any of the waltzes, through a series of dances and dramatic tableaux, to a complex coda that integrates all the thematic material except that of the introduction in a brilliant finale. The work starts with a long, soft trill in the right hand, which sets the scene, but is ambiguous until the left hand enters with a sequence of chords. This time they are not a call to the dancers but a suggestion of a musical sound heard from afar: of an orchestra tuning up, or perhaps one heard by a listener approaching the room where it is playing.

Then the swirling waltz itself bursts in, like a ballroom scene in a film by a great director. The sense is not that the listener is dancing, but rather watching dancers as they circle the room. Chopin creates this spinning effect by playing three rhythms off one another: the familiar "oom-pah-pah" waltz bass in the left hand, a melody in two-note phrases that are unusual for this dance, and a series of steady running notes in between. The second theme is a brilliant racing figure that returns importantly throughout the work, particularly in the closing; then a few other waltz tunes follow, again creating the sense that the listener is attending a ball and watching a series of scenes.

The middle of the work contains the first private conversation in the waltzes, in which Chopin musically portrays dancers talking to each other in the intimacy of the dance. This builds to an impassioned climax, which gives way to the racing figure, then the two-note tune, and then another big climax introducing the coda, where the racing figure takes over, hurrying this extraordinary, forward-looking musical drama to a blazing finish.

The three Waltzes of op. 64 are masterworks from 1847, Chopin's last productive year before tuberculosis sapped his creative energy. More compact than the ambitious dances of opp. 18, 34, and 42, these works possess the greatest musical and emotional profundity of all. The set opens with the most famous of the waltzes and one of the best known of Chopin's compositions: the "Minute" Waltz, so named for its brevity, although most performances take between ninety seconds and two minutes. It opens with the right hand playing a busy spinning sequence, with which the left hand finally catches up, turning the little blizzard of notes into a melody that reaches up to a high note held just a bit longer than the surrounding bustle. This forms the emotional peak of this first section, which for all its grace betrays an underlying urgency, perhaps even anxiety. The middle section features a right-hand melody that starts conventionally but quickly flutters as though out of breath, undermined as well by a jumpy left hand part. The repeat of the second theme is more stable and elegantly decorated. A long trill, much like the one that opens op. 42, leads to a reprise of the first part; and the piece is over, indeed almost before the listener knows it, in a long, graceful scale rushing down the keyboard.

The second Waltz, in C-sharp minor (track 7 on the CD), is nearly as well known and loved as its predecessor in the op. 64 set. It opens without introduction, plunging directly into its famous tune, bittersweet (but more bitter than sweet) and with a curious rhythmic tic that sounds more like speech than dance. The second part of the theme (0:14) consists chiefly of sequences of notes in a steady rhythm moving up, reaching a peak at 0:17, and then coming down. This too evokes dialogue rather than dance.

The theme is immediately repeated in a condensed form (0:22), leading to the second theme (0:48), one of Chopin's great inspirations. Marked *piu mosso*—more quickly—this infinitely graceful and melancholy tune suggests whirling dancers at some kind of distance, perhaps in another room or at another time. It is repeated more softly (1:03), its rising scale and fade-out leading to the third theme in a consoling major key and slower tempo. The waltz rhythm all but disappears as the right hand plays an impassioned, speechlike sequence notable for its confessional quality. This melody reaches its high point at 1:31 and then descends, to be repeated eloquently ornamented (1:38 through 1:55), when the left hand undermines the right by taking on a different rhythm. At 2:03 the graceful, faraway waltz comes back, played exactly as it was the first time and then (2:18) repeated softly again. The opening group returns at 2:30, played just as it was at the beginning. Then (3:22) the quick waltz comes back once more to bring the piece to an end, which it does without flourish, instead dying softly away on a rising scale (3:44).

While it would be foolish to dream up characters or situations for the three themes of the C-sharp minor Waltz, each one, quite different from its companions, is instantly recognizable. The second theme, that sweeping waltz tune, acts as a frame for the entire composition. It is the most frequently recurring, memorable, and impersonal of the three. The opening theme and the middle section are intimate utterances of radically different personalities, making a sense of contrast and even conflict between them inevitable. There is no room in this profound and personal work for rhetorical gestures, such as an introduction or a coda. If it falls short of tragic stature, the pain it conveys is all too clear. The C-sharp minor Waltz is uncomplicated in form. Its power derives from the way Chopin plays its distinctly different themes against one other, thereby creating a dramatic scenario of startling poignancy.

Much less popular than its companions in the op. 64 set, the third Waltz in A-flat major is just as great and the most musically advanced of the three. But it is also the least waltzlike, containing irregularities that take it well into the realm of the abstract and a middle section that is closer to a mazurka in its rhythmic and melodic profiles. The work begins directly with a statement of the melody, which displays a specific kind of slippery sound known as *chromaticism* and refuses to stay in its home key—or *any* key—for long. The melody finally spreads out and dissolves into two long trills, followed by a highly unconventional melodic phrase in which the piano seems to acquire speech.

The middle section, in a distant key, carries the melody heard in the previous passage into the bass, accompanied by chords in the right hand that are rhythmically steady but shift in a rainbow of dark harmonies. Now Chopin removes any semblance of regularity from the phrasing of the left-hand melody, breaking up the right-hand rhythm and then pushing the harmony to ever more remote areas. Chopin finds his way with elegant speed to the opening theme, but again changes the key to a very distant one, then back again to A-flat major, as a coda based on passages heard near the beginning bring this dense and daring work to an end. The harmonic adventures of later composers as different as Wagner and Debussy owe an immense debt to Chopin for a groundbreaking work like this.

The remaining six waltzes of the fourteen of the standard canon were all published after Chopin's death. Composed between 1829 and 1842, they embrace most of Chopin's creative maturity, covering his early and middle stylistic periods. The Waltz in A-flat major (Chopin's clear favorite as a key for waltzes), op. 69, no. 1, is a work from 1835 sometimes nicknamed "L'Adieu"—the farewell—because of its slow tempo and melancholy mood. It is built from only two themes—the first of which is a passionate operatic melody, slightly varied in its several recurrences—and a rising chordal theme that contrasts with the opening melody but has a similar upward reach. Both themes have a speechlike quality that takes this sad and beautiful work far from the dance floor.

The companion work in B minor, dating from 1829, is built out of three themes: the first a sinuous figure for the right hand, the second with a different rhythmic profile, and the third in B major, consisting of a twisting figure much like the opening theme, combined with another component based on a rhythm that hops more like a mazurka than a waltz. The feel of this dance seems more Polish than Parisian.

If the B minor Waltz resembles a mazurka, then the G-flat major Waltz, op. 70, no. 1, composed in 1835, has a strong Viennese flavor. This short three-part waltz opens directly with an almost dizzying tune in a fast tempo (*molto vivace*—very lively) reminiscent of yodeling; some of Schubert's dances are built of similar figures that also sweep rapidly up and then down the keyboard. The slower middle section offers a tasty imitation of Austrian schmalz. The opening theme returns to bring this unabashedly cheerful work—a rare commodity in Chopin's output—to an end.

The F minor Waltz, op. 70, no. 2, from 1842, is far more complex than its predecessor. It moves at moderate speed, and its minor key signature guarantees a more somber tone. The first theme starts in a restricted range reminiscent of a vocal melody but soon widens to include jumps that are only possible on an instrument. The rhythm is softly understated, and the harmony—which shifts between major and minor, and from the home key to A-flat major—is intricate and rich. The F minor Waltz is also an interesting experiment in form, in which the brief second theme seems to grow out of the opening one. The second theme also returns just before the end, which is quiet and devoid of rhetoric.

The last two waltzes are great works from Chopin's early period. The D-flat major Waltz, op. 70, no. 3, is a lovely dance that displays Chopin's matchless grasp of keyboard writing and in some ways looks ahead to the mature waltzes. This idealized waltz, which reflects its early date of composition by its multiplicity of themes, consists of four short dances arranged in mirror form. It opens with an exquisite and wistful dance in which melodic lines interweave in a way unimaginable on any instrument other than the piano. The graceful motion of the second theme is also conceived pianistically. In the third section, the right hand takes over the waltz rhythm, while the left takes the melody. The luscious second theme concludes the piece.

The E minor Waltz, op. posthumous, composed in 1830, is a near-masterpiece that has always been popular. It displays a fantastic rhythmic energy that gives it perhaps the greatest sense of impetus of any of these works. The fierce swirl of the opening passage seems not so much a call to the dance floor as another cinematic evocation of a ballroom scene. Here, matters proceed at breathtaking speed, from the crisply articulated repeated notes of the first theme through the sparkling middle section—which provides a change of key to E major but moves at the same headlong pace—and through to the cathartic summing-up of the short coda.

Chopin's waltzes are less popular today than they were fifty years ago. It was then common for pianists to program all fourteen as the second half of a recital program. In the late nineteenth and early twentieth centuries, the masterworks of Chopin that were overtly masculine, such as the F-sharp minor Polonaise, op. 44 (track 10 on the CD), or difficult to interpret and understand, such as the F minor Ballade, op. 52 (track 16), were neglected in favor of the waltzes. And ironically, some critics of a century ago carped that Chopin's music was too "feminine." Today the pendulum has swung from the Chopin of the once-beloved waltzes to the composer of the mighty polonaises, sonatas, scherzos, and ballades, and the concentrated, modernist mazurkas and preludes. But the waltzes themselves have lost none of their beauty and power of invention.

Operatic Reveries
The Nocturnes

Chopin was neither the first composer nor the last to write nocturnes, but he was surely the greatest. Chopin's nocturnes are works of tremendous power, more like miniature operas—some including ballets—than the wistful, slow pieces the title suggests.

All discussions of Chopin's nocturnes necessarily mention John Field (1782–1837), the Irish-born composer and pianist who was his chief forerunner as a composer in the genre. Field, a traveling musician and virtuoso—who lived most of his adult life in Russia and was much admired, as Chopin would later be, for his delicacy of touch at the keyboard—composed seventeen or eighteen nocturnes, depending on whether one counts a nocturnelike work entitled *Midi*. Field's nocturnes are lyrical character pieces in which melodies like those of Italian opera and French songs of the era float above rippling accompaniments. The banal tunes, thin and repetitious accompaniments, and unadventurous harmony of Field's nocturnes combine to produce an overall effect that is pleasant but pallid, with boredom setting in quickly when listening even to one.

That these watery little pieces influenced Chopin seems unquestionable, but Chopin's earliest nocturne (in E minor, published posthumously as op. 72, no. 1) far surpasses Field's best effort. This work, composed in 1827, displays the characteristics of Chopin's heroic vision of the nocturne: the slow or moderate speed, sweeping left hand accompaniment, and passionate, intense melody, inspired by Italian opera.

Such melodies—idealized, sculpted transfigurations of those Chopin heard in the works of Rossini and Bellini—dominate the nocturnes.

Chopin's profound sympathy with the Italian operatic style allowed him to transfer its large melodic spans and potent emotional content to the piano, which cannot sing but for which Chopin devised a sound that evokes the voice. Nowhere is Chopin's obsession with vocally styled *legato*—tying notes together seamlessly—more apparent than in the long-spun, passionate melodies of the nocturnes. Unlike the voice (and string and wind instruments as well), the piano is an elaborate percussion mechanism incapable of true legato. A good pianist's legato is an illusion, brought about by his or her skilled deployment of fingers, hand, and wrist, and artifice in the use of the piano's sustain pedal. Chopin's students were unanimous in describing his obsession with legato: he advised some to take singing lessons (he is quoted as saying, "you must sing if you wish to play") to help them understand how it *feels* to connect notes; virtually all were told to model their melodic phrasing on that of the great singers of the day. In their dramatic scenarios and operatic melodies, the nocturnes are the high point of Chopin's metabolic conversion of the Italian vocal style to the keyboard.

The E minor Nocturne, supposedly composed just after the death of Chopin's sister Ludwika, shares an elegiac quality with many of the later nocturnes. As in most of the nocturnes, the left hand in the E minor work plays chords that have been broken apart into individual notes (arpeggios) that in this case sweep grandly up and down the keyboard. Unlike Field's, this tune, played by the right hand, burns quickly into the memory. It droops; then rises; then moves to two notes, reminiscent of two voices in an operatic duet; then returns richly ornamented—displaying throughout this astonishingly mature work by the seventeen-year-old genius a riveting tension and force.

The next three nocturnes, published in 1832 as Chopin's op. 9, are powerful, original, and technically finished. Along with the contemporaneous mazurkas of opp. 6 and 7, they represent the earliest works by the fully mature composer. (As with the mazurkas, Chopin worked in the nocturne form throughout his career). The first of the set, in B-flat minor, opens with a mournful melody over a flowing left hand that is Chopin's expansion of a specific type of arpeggio accompaniment known as the Alberti bass. The middle section is hypnotic, with remarkable harmonic shifts over a droning bass line that adds a touch of mystery. The original melancholy tune returns, lavishly ornamented, to bring the work to an atmospheric end.

Named for the eighteenth-century musician who devised it, the Alberti bass consists of a three-note chord broken into a flowing stream of notes (most typically, first the lowest, then the highest, then the middle, and then the highest again) played by the left hand as accompaniment to the melody in the right, carrying the harmony and moving in a steady rhythm and pace. One famous example from among countless that could be cited is that which supports the opening melody of Mozart's Piano Sonata in C major, K. 545. To say the Alberti bass was much favored by composers throughout the classical era, including Mozart, Haydn, Beethoven, and Schubert, is an understatement: it became a genuine musical convention, the bread-and-butter melodic accompaniment of the age.

Obviously by Chopin's time it was hardly original, but neither can it be called trite: the very neutrality of the figure kept—and keeps—it from cloying, and it is marvelously adaptable. Depending on the tune above, its rippling motion can convey urgency as well as profound calm. Even the Viennese giants left the Alberti bass pretty much as they found it, Beethoven employing it as late as 1814 in the Sonata no. 27 in E minor, op. 90, and Schubert in his final piano sonata, the mighty B-flat major of 1828. But writers of opera, notably Bellini, adapted the Alberti bass for orchestral use to accompany arias. It is in the style of Bellini's broadened version, rather than the keyboard works of the Viennese school, that Chopin took this musical commonplace, opening its relatively tight range of notes to a wider, richer, and more expressive span from deep in the keyboard to well up into its middle range, complementing the large melodic scale on which he worked. He would employ this vastly expanded descendent of the Alberti bass to great effect throughout his career, particularly to accompany and amplify passionate, operatically inspired tunes.

The second Nocturne of op. 9, in E-flat, is the most famous of all and one of the simplest. In it, a familiar, tranquil tune floats above an accompaniment in a light waltz rhythm that Chopin employs again in two other nocturnes. The melody is restated with heavy ornamental incrustation and then again more plainly before a magnificent flourish guides the work to its conclusion. This piece, once so popular that it became hackneyed, is now rarely performed except in complete recordings of the nocturnes. While it may be one of the lesser works in the series, a good performance is quite effective, and it does contain early examples of ideas and writing Chopin would later use to greater effect in the nocturnes as well as in other forms.

The third Nocturne of op. 9, in B major, is a different sort of work altogether. Cut on a larger scale than either of its companions, this strange piece moves at a more animated pace. The opening tune, in an operatic style but marked *scherzando* (playful), might be called full-throated except for its dancelike restlessness. The left hand plays an unusual blend of a light waltz rhythm with the Alberti bass. The tune is repeated with delicate but nervous ornamentation, before a blustering middle section in B minor intrudes. The opening melody comes back again, reaching an unambiguously operatic climax on a powerful high note, followed by another glorious rainbow of decoration just before the end. Here Chopin slows the tempo, bringing the work to a peaceful conclusion that feels hard won after the tension of what went before.

The three Nocturnes of op. 15 appear to have been conceived at the same time as those of op. 9, but they were published separately in 1833. They share a compact three-part structure but are as bold and forward-looking as their predecessors. The first Nocturne, in F major, starts with a delicate melody so deeply Italian in feeling that it seems folklike, more boatman's song or lullaby than aria. The left hand plays a gentle, lilting light-waltz rhythm. The piano sound has an almost pastel-like quality, until the start of the violent middle section, which blasts away all traces of the opening. This aggressive interruption sounds like a study for the second theme of the F major Ballade, op. 38, which has a similar rhythmic pattern and intrudes just as abruptly. But the opening section comes back as though nothing had happened, ending the work quietly.

Opera is clearly the inspiration for the opening melody of the F-sharp major Nocturne, op. 15, no. 2. This drooping melody, heavily encrusted with ornamentation at every appearance, has an overripe, decadent quality unlike that of any other tune by Chopin. The middle section is swiftly flowing and agitated, and the reprise of the opening section leads to a climax on a high note, followed by the first of several long, elaborate codas in the nocturnes with the shuddering rhythm of a leaf's dying fall.

The last Nocturne of the set, in G minor, is a distinctive mood piece that is rarely heard in live performance. Its intimate, personal character is not well suited for the concert hall. It opens with a contained melody over an odd, limping accompaniment; the harmony contains some striking dissonances. This gradually builds to a climax, followed by a middle section consisting of churchlike chords, marked *religioso*. The third section grows out of the second but is of different material. Chopin clearly had some scenario in mind when he wrote this unusual nocturne, but extramusical guessing games serve no purpose.

The C-sharp minor Nocturne that opens op. 27, published in 1836, is the first large-scale masterpiece in the series. Here the dramatic inspiration is magnificently obvious; but instead of an Italian-style melody, a wailing, Asiatic theme clashes sharply with the harmony of the droning left hand accompaniment, creating an extraordinary setting suggestive of night, mystery, and menace. In the middle section, the tempo picks up as sharply accented chords thunder over racing left-hand figuration. This builds to a massive passage marked *appassionato,* a sudden and shocking change of key, and an ecstatic climax. While the music tells no specific story, the violence it conveys is unmistakable. The last page brings back the mysterious opening—now powerfully suggestive of a return to an earlier scene or setting, but in a different light following the ferocity of the middle section—and a shift into the major key that brings little relief. Chopin's sense of dramatic pacing in this tightly structured work is equal to that of any opera composer's.

The second Nocturne of op. 27, in D-flat major (track 8 on the CD), is one of Chopin's greatest and most beautiful tributes to the Italian opera, especially to the work of his friend and colleague Vincenzo Bellini, whose inimitable melodies have been the envy of many composers. Chopin here writes a love duet in Bellini's style, adapted with absolute sureness to the piano.

The work opens with the left hand stating the broken-chord figure that will run through the entire piece: an Alberti bass that is highly evolved from its modest ancestor. Instead of covering a tight range of notes, this jumps from deep in the bass up into the center of the keyboard, creating a rich and mellow sonority. Chopin uses this unending, steady flow to comment on and enrich the busy melodic activity of the right hand; gorgeous as that will be, the left hand shares the stage, holding its own as a nearly equal partner. It is worthwhile to compare the left-hand writing in this piece to that of the A-flat major Etude, op. 25, no. 1, first on the CD. While the melodies and left-hand figurations are laid out differently, both accompaniments contribute texture and harmony. Chopin's unparalleled understanding of the piano allowed him to mine the instrument for all the expressiveness it can offer—a long way from the dry little accompaniment conceived by Domenico Alberti.

The melody enters (0:04), arching gracefully down, then up, then down again, pausing briefly (0:20) as a singer would for breath. This heroically beautiful tune, richly decorated with grace notes and the lavish runs known in vocal music as *fiorature* (flowerings), imprints itself easily on the mind. At 0:27 it reaches upward for its first high note. At 0:37 a second voice joins. Both are played by the right hand, as the left continues its steady flow. In an operatic duet, this would be the voice of the tenor joining the soprano. The entwined voices continue their richly ornamented course until 1:16, when they separate into a series of phrases more like *recitative* (the word for sung prose or dialogue). But at no time has the texture changed from pianistic—the runs and decorations are no slavish imitations of singing but rather a loving tribute to operatic style, re-created for the keyboard with transcendent skill.

The recitative-like section fades gently (1:37) into a series of long-held single notes, marked *sempre legatissimo*—extremely legato throughout—as the opening tune returns at 1:53. It reaches for the high note again at 2:19, followed by a dizzying spray of notes powerfully suggestive of a great soprano's fioratura but beyond the capability of the human voice, displaying once more Chopin's twin inspirations of Italianate melody and the resources of the piano. This leads to the long, ecstatic duet at the center of the work, reaching what sounds like a fiery exchange of vows, beginning at 3:07 and ending in a long, forceful downward run at 3:20. Note also the way the left hand makes its presence heard in the deep first notes of the six-note bass figures, such as at 3:08 and 3:12. The opening melody makes its final appearance at 3:24; there is a dizzying run at 3:48, followed at 4:01 by another duet passage. Chopin's markings here are important to the passionate quality of the work: *con anima*—with soul; *con fuoco*—with fire; and finally *appassionato,* as the climax is reached in a display reminiscent of fireworks soaring, exploding quietly, and then falling (4:31 through 4:38).

Now the long, glorious coda begins (4:46) with a two-note dipping figure, repeated five times and then again, but now decorated (5:03). The work moves toward a serene ending with an astonishing passage in which the two "voices" in the right hand chant imitative passages, sounding once more like a soprano and tenor in the closing moments of their declaration of eternal love. This masterpiece ends on a mellifluous passage in which the two voices soar upward in sweet harmony (5:45), the steady left-hand accompaniment finally coming to rest as well.

Chopin conceived the ten nocturnes that followed on a scale as large as or larger than the op. 27 works. They were published in sets of two—the next pair, op. 32, coming out in 1837. The first of these, in B major, is yet another operatic takeoff, opening with a tranquil melody that is interrupted by a brief but dramatic pause. The melody continues almost imperturbably, with exquisite ornamentation and a complementary second tune, suggestive of another voice, as in the D-flat major Nocturne. But the ominous pause also appears three more times, each occurrence more unsettling than the one before. There is an abrupt change of harmony and a throbbing in the bass, followed by a series of impassioned declarations interspersed with sharply accented chords that are a direct imitation of an operatic dialogue in recitative, in a shocking ending that is surely dramatic and perhaps tragic.

The second Nocturne of the set, in A-flat major, is more a blend of song and dance, framed by a passage of beautiful arpeggiated chords. The first section is built of a long, memorable, vocally styled melody over a lilting, light waltz accompaniment, which, however, adds considerable interest to the harmony. This gives way to a middle section in a more forceful rhythm that sounds like a ballet—this nocturne has in fact been choreographed. The big tune of the first section returns, more and more decorated, as the broken chords bring this fine work to a rounded and satisfying conclusion.

The G minor Nocturne that is the first of the op. 37 pair (published in 1840) seems a recasting of the op. 15, no. 3, Nocturne in the same key. There are some differences—including a rhythm that is reminiscent of a funeral march rather than the curious, limping waltz of the earlier work—and a more conventionally operatic melody, but both feature chordal middle sections with a processional quality. Taken on its own, this nocturne is fine music and certainly beautifully crafted, but it lacks the grip and weird power of its G minor predecessor.

The G major Nocturne that follows is, on the other hand, one of the greatest of the series. This beautiful and graceful music is also fantastically bold, showing a distinct influence on later composers, perhaps most notably in the piano music of the Frenchmen Debussy and Fauré. It is actually a *barcarolle,* the Italian boatman's song with a rocking rhythm that Chopin took to its absolute peak in his work of that title published as op. 60 (examined in chapter 8), which itself bears many resemblances to a nocturne but is larger in scale. This barcarolle-nocturne opens gently in the left hand, with the right entering quickly and sweetly with a rippling figure suggestive of the movement of a small boat being propelled through the water. Almost from the beginning, the harmony shifts and shimmers daringly, perhaps depicting light on the water; like water, the harmony in this work is never still. The melody is also phrased in an uncommon pattern of three bars rather than the usual four or eight.

The second section is set in a rocking long–short pattern typical of the barcarolle. The opening figure is heard once more, then the rocking theme, this time made gripping by a subversive, side-slipping harmonic movement. Chopin uses the same rhythmic pattern and slipping harmony to great effect in the Ballade in F minor, op. 52, composed three years later, and in the Barcarolle, op. 60, of 1846. The rippling opening returns; then, after a pause, the piece fades out on the rocking figure. As with many of the mazurkas, the G major Nocturne's instabilities and irregularities give the music a delicious piquancy.

The epic Nocturne in C minor, op. 48, no. 1, is the most massive and powerful of the series, structurally and emotionally resembling the ballades and scherzos as much as it does the other nocturnes. It also shares with the C-sharp minor Nocturne of op. 27 an inescapable sense of drama: a tragic scenario clearly unfolds over the course of its six pages. This colossal piece opens with an imploring melody that coils and uncoils upon itself with an almost Bachian intensity over the solemn tread of a funeral march. The harmony changes to C major, and the tempo slows as both hands play a long series of huge murmuring chords, eventually interspersed with powerful rumblings. This builds to a vast, quasi-orchestral climax in thundering octaves, which lead into a recapitulation of the opening but in a quicker, more agitated tone and accompanied by trembling figuration in both hands. In a good performance, this section will sound passionate; in a great one, devastated.

If the C minor Nocturne is red hot, then its companion in F-sharp minor sounds marvelously cool in comparison. Its instrumentally conceived opening section offers a long, gracefully descending melody over a swaying accompaniment. This is the longest of all the nocturnes, but it moves at a flowing pace that never drags. It has a large central section—suggestive of operatic recitative—and one of Chopin's most beautiful codas, an exquisite dying fall that moves into the consoling major key at the end.

The Nocturnes of op. 55 are transitional works: the first of the set, in F minor, belongs to Chopin's middle period, while the second, in E-flat major, shares with the op. 62 Nocturnes and the op. 60 Barcarolle a visionary quality. The F minor work opens with a funeral march that is lyrical and without a trace of pomp, followed by another of Chopin's acutely observed, operatically styled recitatives. A fleet middle section moves directly into a long, beautiful coda in which the opening melody is broken into a flowing rhythm, leading seamlessly into a passage where the harmony spreads into a glorious rainbow of piano sound that is one of the composer's trademarks.

This subtle, understated work seems a bit neglected among its grand companions. With the E-flat major Nocturne that is the second of the op. 55 pair, Chopin returns to Italian operatic melody as his inspiration. The work, a highly evolved descendant of op. 9, no. 2, is in the same key and built on one theme as well. But in eleven years, Chopin had learned how to fuse all the elements into a profound whole. This is a densely woven musical fabric in which the listener hears the soaring melody and sweeping accompaniment as one; the harmony is fantastically rich, and most of the ornamentation here is intrinsic to the melodic line rather than a decorative overlay. Chopin, that great student of the music of Bach, weaves these strands together in a manner that shows his consummate mastery of counterpoint. This transcendent music shares with Chopin's final works, most notably the op. 62 Nocturnes, an inward fire and purity of spirit.

That final pair of nocturnes are majestic utterances in Chopin's final style—the equivalent of *Die Zauberflöte* in Mozart's body of work, the late string quartets in Beethoven's, and *Parsifal* in Wagner's. All share a beauty that seems idealized and unearthly: purged of flesh, musically complex, sometimes painfully abstract.

The B major Nocturne, op. 62, no. 1, opens with a grandly arpeggiated chord, followed by one of Chopin's purest bel canto melodies, interwoven with an accompaniment that is a sophisticated offspring of the simple Alberti bass. This melody, unlike other operatically inspired tunes in the nocturnes, sits well within singable range. The middle section, in a remote key, is also vocal, and set over a gloriously complex accompaniment that still has a free, almost improvisatory quality. Now the opening melody comes back in visionary form, intensified by burning trills. The harmony moves through some of Chopin's most daring modulations, and the work ends with a long, magnificent dying-fall coda and a final series of three recitative-like phrases.

The last Nocturne, in E major, op. 62, no. 2, opens directly with a grandly proportioned melody that sounds as though it might have come straight out one of Bellini's operas. This ripe tune sits, like the melody of its predecessor, within vocal range, at least until more pianistic decoration takes over. There is an ecstatic second theme over a gently running left hand that builds gradually to a middle section, marked *agitato*. Here Chopin's writing is purely instrumental. The agitation seems idealized, however, and far above any specific worldly grief. The first theme returns once more, in all its radiance, and then the second, ecstatic theme turns into a coda. Chopin's last nocturne ends on yet one more "sung," recitative-like phrase.

Opera is one of Western music's major achievements, deriving its power from the direct expression of emotion by that most potent of all instruments, the human voice. Feelings are distilled into melodies, conceived to penetrate the listener's heart and mind, from which they cannot be dislodged—the most outstanding example perhaps being "La donna è mobile" from Verdi's *Rigoletto*. Liszt cranked out plenty of potpourris for piano based on famous operatic tunes, filled with love for the source material but none displaying the profound sensitivity to the voice shown by Chopin in the D-flat major Nocturne. The best way to feel the immeasurable impact of Italian opera and why it has spoken with such force to musicians and laymen is simply to listen to Rossini, Bellini, Donizetti, and Verdi, the culminating figures of this mighty tradition. Chopin knew the work of Rossini and Bellini well; genuine understanding of his output demands immersion in the works of these masters. There are those who scorn Italian opera as a vulgar entertainment, but like most musicians, Chopin knew better.

6 *The Sonatas*

In Italian, *sonata* means nothing more than "sounded," signifying by extension a sounded piece of music—what other kind could there be? Neutral but misleading, this deadly little term covers the widest range of instrumental compositions imaginable, as well as musical structures that lie at the heart of the classical tradition. Baroque masters from Corelli to Bach composed sonatas, none in "sonata form"; neither are the 550 or so for keyboard by Domenico Scarlatti (1685–1757). These brilliant works, character pieces, and technical studies, mostly in a straightforward two-part form, seem to have been much admired by Chopin.

Haydn's astonishing application of classical sonata form can be found throughout the first movements of his instrumental music, including the symphonies, the vast range of his chamber music, and the daring, eccentric, neglected piano sonatas. The first movements of most of these works present two themes of contrasting character, the first usually brisk or aggressive, the second lyrical. These are put into conflict, picked apart, redistributed, and combined before being guided back home to the opening theme and key, but Haydn's passion for surprise and shock place these movements among his most spectacularly unstable. Mozart's acute dramatic sense allowed him to use the conflict inherent in sonata form to find in his instrumental works emotional depths approaching those probed in his operas. As with most musical structures he touched, Beethoven could not leave the sonata or sonata form the way he found it. The dramatic conflicts of his symphonies are well known, and the other instrumental forms he worked in, from string quartet to piano sonata, were changed irrevocably by his contact. Beethoven's thirty-two piano sonatas include some of his greatest works, covering the full range of his styles—from the brisk early works, rooted firmly in the classical tradition, to the unearthly spirituality of the final three sonatas. Moreover, there is within the series an astonishing variety, with no two built the same way.

Thus, the sonata tradition was already fairly loose by the time Chopin got to it in 1827. His own view of Beethoven seems to have consisted more of admiration than love, but his clear favorite among that master's piano sonatas was the A-flat major, op. 26, an unconventional work that opens not with a sonata movement but with a set of slow variations on a lyrical theme; its third movement, like that of Chopin's B-flat minor Sonata, is a funeral march. Chopin played and taught the work repeatedly, clearly learning much from it. Chopin's sonatas are likewise not off the ready-to-wear rack, in line with his tendency to make radical alterations to existing forms and to create new ones as he needed them. Music critics used to decry Chopin's modifications to the sonata, tiresomely—and incorrectly—citing these as examples of his inability to build musical structures on a large scale. Today such complaints are mostly discredited, and the sonatas are admired for their daring and experimental qualities.

Chopin composed five works in sonata form: the three piano sonatas (no. 1 in C minor, op. 4; no. 2 in B-flat minor, op. 35; and no. 3 in B minor, op. 58), the Sonata for Piano and Cello, op. 65, and the Trio in G minor, op. 8. The first Sonata, a complex and very difficult student work from 1827 and '28 that fails to coalesce, and the Trio (1829) are played almost never; the Cello Sonata is a great work heard only occasionally; and the second and third Sonatas are among the most popular works in the virtuoso repertory.

The B-flat minor Sonata opens with a grave and urgent question posed by the left hand; then a churning figure accompanies the first theme, which is plaintive, breathless, and desperate. The second theme, built of calm chords in D-flat major, follows, leading directly to a glorious, operatic climax over wide-ranging arpeggios in the left hand. This is followed by a page of great technical difficulty: big handfuls of chords that move swiftly up and down the keyboard.

Early in the work's published life, a serious mistake entered most printed editions of the text, taking the first movement's main theme as the start of the repeat; most pianists, including some of the greatest, have played the work with the mistake despite its egregious and un-Chopin-like awkwardness. Both Brahms, who edited the Chopin sonatas, and the contemporary musicologist and pianist Charles Rosen understood that the repeat actually begins with the solemn opening passage. When played this way—as still, for some reason, few pianists other than Rosen do—the structure of the movement makes perfect sense. In any case, if the repeat is observed, this is where it occurs, but it is far better omitted altogether than played with the gauche error.

The next section (the *development* in standard sonata form) begins with the opening melody treated as a rhythmic figure for the left hand that sounds like an exhausted swimmer trying to touch bottom, interspersed with a version of the chordal second subject. These are combined and built into one of Chopin's greatest, most beautiful, and most terrifying passages: a visionary moment at the brink that sounds like the beating of vast and awful wings. Such transcendence cannot last, subsiding to a more lyrical but still troubled episode, which returns the listener to the second subject and its passionate climax. The coda of this titanic movement opens with the murderous chordal sequence, leading into another breathless passage in which the left hand plays the galloping rhythm of the opening theme beneath a sequence of massive, proto-Wagnerian chords.

The second movement is called a *scherzo,* a form in which Chopin composed four of his most important works, examined in chapter 9. Unlike the four independent scherzos, which are freestanding, the scherzo of the B-flat minor Sonata is linked intimately with the movements that precede and follow it. Although this movement might be able to stand on its own in performance, the unity of this tightly conceived four-movement work would be destroyed without it. Seeming to grow directly from the rhythmic figure that ended the first movement, this is a large-scale dance in a clattering mazurka rhythm. Listeners hoping for comfort after the terrors of the opening movement will be disappointed: this jarring, heavy-footed dance is interspersed with ominous rising chromatic figures. The middle section does, however, feature a warm, Bellinian melody over a gently throbbing bass and another of Chopin's tributes to the cello, where the melody passes smoothly into the left hand. But soon the clangorous mazurka returns. The ending of the movement brings back the operatic melody of the middle section, and the movement ends inconclusively with a bump in the bass.

The third movement (or at least its opening phrase) is Chopin's most famous piece by far. Nevertheless, the Funeral March is gripping: as the keystone of the sonata, it deserves a hearing with open ears. That opening phrase, oppressively heavy, is repeated immediately, intensifying its somber effect. This leads to a magnificent upward-thrusting passage ending with trills in imitation of drum rolls; Chopin will create another, even greater impression of rattling drums in the F-sharp minor Polonaise, op. 44, track 10 on the CD. (The Funeral March of Beethoven's op. 26 Sonata has comparable passages, evoking rumbling drums and salvos of an artillery salute). The long middle section, which consists of a noble floating tune that can sound banal when played too loosely and softly, is another takeoff on Bellini's elegiac style, but with its own still and meditative feel. The opening section returns to end the movement in the blackest gloom.

The finale (track 9 on the CD) is built entirely of rushing figuration in a steady rhythmic pattern, played very quietly until a crash at the end. The hands play in unison, an octave apart, with no harmonization except for what is occasionally suggested by the ear based on notes it has just heard. Although it begins in B-flat minor, the music drifts away from the home key toward atonality, making it hard to find something musically conventional to hold on to. The effect is profoundly unsettling, even terrifying. There is a two-part structure, again difficult to pick out due to the music's melodic and harmonic featurelessness. For these reasons, this eeriest of sonata finales does not lend itself to a blow-by-blow description; better just to let the ninety seconds of it wash over you in all its weirdness.

Technically and structurally, the movement bears a resemblance to some of the preludes: no. 14 in E-flat minor most of all and no. 19 in E-flat major as well. But its placement within the structure of the sonata gives it greater weight than either piece from op. 28, concluding this fearsome and courageous work with a harshness past tragedy. The movement stands far beyond what even the most sympathetic audience of 1840 would have grasped and remains difficult listening—on many levels—today. Even as astute a critic as Robert Schumann found it difficult to swallow, writing that Chopin had "yoked four of his strangest and most heterogeneous children together to make a Sonata." Repulsed particularly by the Funeral March and the finale, Schumann wrote: "From this musical line without melody and without joy, there breathes a strange, horrible spirit which annihilates with its heavy fist anything that resists it, and we listen with fascination and without protesting until the end—but without, nevertheless, being able to praise: for this is not music." The usually brave Schumann was put off by the starkness of this death-haunted sonata, built by Chopin around the Funeral March composed two years earlier in 1837. Just as puzzling in its way is the sonata's popularity today, not easily explained given its gloomy character. The work is played often in recital and recorded regularly by virtuosi, although rarely well; a great performance is bound to be disturbing.

The Sonata no. 3 in B minor, op. 58, composed in 1844, is one of the high-water marks of Chopin's musical maturity. Grand in conception and noble in expression, the B minor Sonata is an outburst of healthy joy and technical mastery that makes it entirely different listening from its great but grim predecessor. The deterioration of Chopin's health and the miseries of his failing relationship with George Sand seem to have no voice in this powerful work: like many artists, he was able to keep his personal life and artistic expression separate.

The sonata opens with a forceful phrase arching downward, replied to by a sequence of rich chords. By the end of the first page, the music shows a distinct tendency to pull away from the home key toward unusual harmonies that will be explored further over the course of the movement. Scales of oceanic vastness sweep the keyboard before the appearance of the second theme in D major, close cousin to the melody of the D-flat major Nocturne, op. 27, no. 2, also placed over a wide-ranging Alberti bass pattern. But the purpose of the tune within the structure of this sonata movement is to provide several contrasts to the opening sequence. To the forthright masculinity of that theme it is "feminine"; moreover, where the first theme is thick, this is songful, balancing the chordal opening with its long-spun, linear melody. Chopin rounds the thematic groups out with a gracious episode ending in arpeggio figurations. These will be brought back to conclude the movement.

The middle section is notable for the density of its counterpoint, the far-ranging harmony, and the proud mastery Chopin exercises over these potentially unruly components, proving himself one of the great musical technicians in these intense, difficult passages. The glorious Bellianian second subject tries, at first with some difficulty, to work its way into the busy proceedings, finally succeeding before the movement is brought triumphantly to a close by the third thematic group.

As with the op. 35 Sonata, Chopin places the scherzo second. This scherzo is unlike any other piece with that title he wrote: instead of the usual somber drama, here all is brisk and bright. And this scherzo could hardly stand on its own; it is, rather, a brief interlude, a light moment in an epic piece. As with the furious Scherzo no. 1, op. 20, the melody of its opening section bubbles up from busy pianistic figuration, although the tone of the two works could hardly differ more. The middle section consists of a more tranquil tune over a lilting accompaniment, reminiscent of the Scherzo no. 4, op. 54, composed the previous year. The slow movement opens thunderously, sounding for a moment like another funeral march, but changes almost immediately into an elegiac and contemplative Italianate melody over a rocking bass. The movement's middle section is long and dreamy with a flowing figuration in the right hand setting an idyllic tone. The Italianate melody returns to end the movement.

The finale is a mighty tour de force, a virtuoso showpiece that is also of great musical substance. It opens with a sweeping passage supercharged with energy, stoking anticipation to a high level. Neither does the main theme disappoint, ranging forward in giant strides with irresistible, driving power. The second theme consists of triumphant chords and runs; as in the first movement, the harmonic shifts are rapid and often unexpected. Throughout the course of the movement, the music bursts with uncontained excitement and athletic vigor, pressing ahead to the conclusion with glittering, often dissonant passagework that presages the work of Fauré, Debussy, and Ravel. This stupendous movement represents the triumph of Chopin's spirit over his frail body.

Chopin composed his Sonata for Piano and Cello in G minor, op. 65, with great difficulty in 1845 and '46. The composer's favorite instrument (after piano and voice) was always the cello; all his chamber works other than the Trio, op. 8 (for piano, violin and cello), had been for piano and cello. This sonata, a great work that has for a number of reasons never found a wide audience, was the result of his close friendship with cellist Auguste Franchomme, with whom Chopin premiered it in 1848. Chamber music has lost popularity since the nineteenth century, when members of aristocratic and bourgeois families performed a wide range of music at home. Today, its matchless repertory is the preserve of the most serious musicians and listeners. The small world of chamber music has its own hierarchy of popularity, and even there, cello sonatas fail to make the top rank. There are just a handful of great works for piano and cello, and while no one would deny Chopin's sonata a place among them, the work has an austerity that sets it apart from the rest of his oeuvre, obvious as its musical merits may be.

The Cello Sonata begins with a grandly proportioned first movement, twice the length of its opposite numbers in opp. 35 and 58. Several very beautiful themes are set forth, with the gloomy opening one dominating. There is some difficult work for the pianist, including a sequence of big, fast-moving chords reminiscent of a passage in the first movement of the B-flat minor Piano Sonata. Among the few consolations in this sorrowful music are a thoughtful chordal theme for the piano and a brief return of the first theme in a rainbow of modulating major keys, but these are brief. As with all of Chopin's music from his late period, the harmony moves rapidly in many different and unexpected directions and the music is tightly developed. But alongside the musical profundity is an inwardness rarely heard in Chopin's music: it does not approach the listener—one must go to it.

The second movement is a scherzo, with a freedom that is welcome after the knotty opening. The middle section contains one of Chopin's great melodies, sung out splendidly by the cello. Yet sadness is palpable even here, despite the more exposed texture and the fire of the outer sections. The slow movement, the shortest in the work, consists of a vast, operatic melody—Chopin's last—shared between the two instruments and spun out in a single, glorious breath. The finale brings back the sober tone and musical complexity of the opening movement. While the sonata ends in the major key, the sense it offers is not of triumph but of struggle. It is that difficulty, along with a pervasive sadness, that keeps the Cello Sonata from wider popularity; nevertheless, this great work always rewards the second, third, fourth, and fifth hearings.

Patriotism and Tragedy
The Polonaises

For Chopin, the polonaise was one of the two vessels (the other being the mazurka) into which he poured his feelings of patriotism and grief over the fall of Poland. Ranking among his mightiest conceptions, the polonaises—gloomy, majestic, warlike, febrile, wild, and proud—are Chopin's tributes to the glory of his conquered homeland. They stand (again, alongside the mazurkas) as perhaps the most important influence on the nationalist schools that followed, including composers as diverse as Liszt, Janáček, Grieg, Falla, Villa Lobos, Vaughan Williams, and Gershwin. It is ironic, in light of Russia's role as Poland's chief oppressor, that Chopin's explicitly patriotic music made its most profound impact on the Russian nationalists, and that the greatest polonaise—perhaps the *only* great polonaise—outside Chopin's oeuvre is by Mussorgsky: in *Boris Godunov,* the apogee of Russian music and one of the towering landmarks of operatic literature. There is a big, pounding polonaise in Tchaikovsky's opera *Euegen Onegin* as well. Nevertheless, Chopin's polonaises still hold their place among the noblest examples of nationalist music.

The dance that would become Chopin's regal polonaise emerged from semicivilized origins in the sixteenth century. Dances with an exotic, Eastern flavor and generic titles ("Polish dance") had their roots in a wide range of folk sources, from song to various types of dance, including what would later develop into the mazurka. By the early eighteenth century, Bach had written several "Polish" dances into his instrumental music, none of which remotely anticipate those of Chopin, although the tune of the polonaise in the Orchestral Suite no. 2 in B minor is apparently based on a Polish folk song. The polacca in the fourth movement of the Brandenburg Concerto no. 1 is a suave little character piece in dance rhythm designed to show off the sound of Bach's string orchestra.

By the late eighteenth century, Polish composers had begun to write polonaises of majestic and melancholy character in response to the partitions of Poland by Russia, Prussia, and Austria. In these little dances, the keys to what would become Chopin's polonaise—chiefly, a stately processional quality and a memorable rhythmic snap—began gradually to coalesce. This characteristic sharply accentuated rhythm (a pattern of notes that goes: long–short–short–long–long–long–long) grips Chopin's polonaises with an obsessive power. The rhythm also found its way to Italy, where it was quickly adopted by operatic composers as a perfect accompaniment to a type of fast aria called a *cabaletta* in dozens of works by composers from Rossini through Verdi.

Polonaises dominate the catalogue of Chopin's earliest compositions: there are half a dozen from the composer's late teens and early twenties that are unheard outside of complete recordings of his music. The one in G minor, composed and published in 1817 by the seven-year-old, is, unsurprisingly, the very first of Chopin's published works, and three charming early works from 1827 and '28 were published posthumously as op. 71. They are rarely heard but make more than satisfactory listening, with the second of the trio, in B-flat major, presenting itself with an appealing youthful swagger.

Chopin's first polonaise published with an opus number is the *Introduction* and *Grande polonaise* in C major, op. 3, for piano and cello. This is what was once known as a "salon piece," to be played before a small audience in the home of wealthy patrons or pupils, whom it was intended only to charm. So it does, with a relaxed, old-fashioned tone and pleasantly virtuosic writing that is not all that difficult for reasonably skilled players.

The *Andante spianato* and *Grande polonaise brillante,* op. 22, is another matter altogether, a pairing of two superb works from 1835 and 1830, respectively. The *Andante spianato* (the last word meaning smooth, which it surely is) has a freedom and openness that makes it seem as though it may have started as an improvisation. Chopin is known to have played this magnificent work not only as a prelude to the polonaise but also on its own to open several of his recitals, preceding pieces of contrasting character. Resembling one of the nocturnes, the G major *Andante spianato,* which Chopin may originally have considered as a third piece for the op. 27 set, is now always followed by the *Grande polonaise brillante.* The once-popular pair, rarely heard in live performance, would still make an excellent program closer, the rapt lyricism of the *Andante spianato* creating anticipation for the athletic polonaise.

The *Andante spianato* opens with one of Chopin's brilliant takes on the Alberti bass, here transformed to a rippling, liquid pulse. The Bellinian melody soon enters in the right hand, clear, soaring and unforgettable. It is immediately restated, exquisitely decorated but never losing its purity of line. A brief interlude that is actually a gentle mazurka, followed by a return of the rippling figuration, draws this gorgeous fantasy lightly to its end, where a tiny memory of the mazurka recurs.

Although the *Andante spianato* is a solo piece, Chopin published the *Grande polonaise brillante* as a concert work for piano and orchestra, with an accompaniment that is small enough for a pianist to cover its few important passages with ease and ignore the rest without the work's suffering. A large-scale virtuoso showpiece, the *Grande polonaise brillante* is well named, expressing unadulterated high spirits that are rare in Chopin's output and not to be found in the other mature polonaises.

The opening theme, set immediately over the characteristic rhythm of the polonaise, is playful, quickly showing a tendency to scamper over the keyboard. Some pianists have said that the work is gratefully written and less difficult to play than it sounds; it certainly sounds hard enough. The first thematic group ends with a dreamy passage. Its second occurrence concludes with thunderous octaves followed by an episode in C minor that is all ardent affect but continues in the same vein of playful sentiment, nobly expressed. Before long, this too bounds off in rapid fingerwork over the sharp polonaise rhythm. The exuberant first theme returns, more heavily decorated, before the start of the coda, which is introduced by a tightening rhythmic sequence similar to the parallel section of the contemporaneous op. 18 Waltz—the *Grande valse brillante.* The coda ends this elegant and aristocratic polonaise in a cascade of notes; the work is a lesson in Chopin's ability to blend lightness with strength without compromising musical content or craftsmanship.

Composed in 1835, the two Polonaises that comprise op. 26 are the first of Chopin's mature canon to speak in heroic and tragic voices. Though these two large-scale works differ radically in tone, they set out the main lines along which the later dances will run. The first, in C-sharp minor, opens with a savagely accented phrase that suggests the galloping of the Polish cavalry, which gives way to a slightly calmer but still proud tune over a brisk cantering rhythm. The second thematic group consists of a tense muttering followed by the quick motion of an upward run. Another fierce episode in the polonaise rhythm follows. So far, all has passed in swift, swirling motion and bright colors, perhaps suggesting uniforms and the thrill of the battlefield. But the long middle section provides contrast, with a more subdued rhythmic profile and considerable subtlety of harmony beneath a tender, vocally styled melody. In another central episode, the beautiful melody passes, cellolike, into the left hand. There is a reprise of the opening group, leading to a brusque ending.

If the C-sharp minor Polonaise conjures up warlike pride, then op. 26, no. 2, in the dark key of E-flat minor, is all bitterness and rage, leading to its nickname "Siberian"—not Chopin's, of course—suggesting Poland's oppression by Russia. This extraordinarily dense and economical work is one of the masterpieces of the composer's early maturity. The tempo indication is *maestoso* (majestic), suggesting a certain gravity and deliberateness.

This Polish tragedy opens with a disturbing series of three softly muttered phrases: the first deep and rumbling, the second the boiled-down essence of the polonaise rhythm in a thickly clotted harmony. This leads into a shrieking climax, followed by an agitated melody in a work built chiefly of rhythm and harmony. The second theme, also in the polonaise rhythm, builds quickly into a series of angry downward runs that balance the scream of the opening page, before collapsing into another chain of muttered phrases that leads into a reprise of the opening. The middle section in B major follows, its martial melody laid closely atop the polonaise rhythm. Filled with nostalgia, it includes an imitation of a drum roll in the left hand. This eventually gives way to a phrase of utter despair, leading back to a brief but complete reiteration of the opening thematic group and a desolate ending. Open in its textures and emotions, the C-sharp minor Polonaise lives on its melodies, while the murmuring and muttering of its companion suggests a terrible interior monologue. The work of a great musical dramatist who never composed an opera, the op. 26 Polonaises reflect gripping dramatic scenarios without lapsing into the banalities of narrative.

The op. 40 pair, composed in 1838 and '39, also offer a contrast: the first piece in A major has been one of the most famous and popular of Chopin's works since its introduction, with the second, in C minor, perpetually in its shadow. The A major Polonaise, nicknamed "Military," is a brilliant piece with an admirable strut. Yet the latter work, richly colored and gloomy, is arguably the greater.

The A major Polonaise opens directly with its famous, stirring theme, presented in bright pomp of daylight. This is the polonaise with the clearest feeling of a processional; to achieve its full grandeur, the music must not move at too quick a pace. A second section replies to the first. Like several of Chopin's polonaise melodies, both carry little rumbling tails. The second section opens with a sharply accented, trumpet-like tune over the thundering polonaise rhythm in the left hand. Chopin puts this proud theme through harmonic changes that soften its outlines just a bit, before a series of fierce trills introduce it once more, played louder yet. The opening theme comes back to bring the work to an end that is triumphant but plain and devoid of rhetoric.

A somber magnificence pervades the opening of the C minor Polonaise, as the stern main theme enters majestically in the left hand beneath pulsing chords in the right. A sorrowful secondary melody grows out of the rich harmony of the right hand's chords, melding with the opening tune. The second section opens with a glorious episode: sharp chords explode in the polonaise rhythm, leading to a magnificent, utterly Chopinesque passage, where the figuration in the right hand is spread by the left hand's harmony into a rainbow of colored aural ribbons.

The more reflective third thematic group, in A-flat major, has a fantastic quality on which Chopin will expand in the opp. 44 and 61 polonaises. Here, the polonaise rhythm is reinterpreted as a series of trumpet calls heard through the shifting harmonies of memory, legend, and dream. Sounding like a full orchestra, the piano writing displays a remarkable richness, as the left hand takes on cellolike figurations that recall the melodic turn of the opening theme, and big, sharply accented chords like those that began the second melodic group. The faraway trumpet calls are heard one last time. They build into a new, rising figure that accompanies the throbbing chords of the opening, and finally the noble theme itself, in a majestic climax that is, however, filled with pain and grief. Few of Chopin's mature works can fairly be thought of as neglected, but the concert-going public would benefit from more frequent performances of this dark-hued masterpiece.

"It's a kind of polonaise but more a fantasia," wrote Chopin about the Polonaise in F-sharp minor, op. 44 (track 10 on the CD). One of the products of the bumper year of 1841, this craggy work is considered by many musicians and critics to be the greatest of the polonaises. Following the lead of op. 40, no. 2, fantasy elements do indeed begin to dominate the content and structure. Formally, this work—one of Chopin's grandest conceptions—is both original and effective, cast in three broad sections, with the outer portions made up of the polonaise and the central episode a mazurka. But Chopin also subdivides the thematic material into smaller groups that help the listener anticipate what is to come by recalling what went before. The F-sharp minor Polonaise includes some of the composer's most nakedly powerful music as well as one of his boldest aural experiments. It contains many savagely repeated patterns that so clearly anticipate the work of Bartók that it would be surprising indeed if that composer did not know it very well. Chopin deliberately limited its palette to metallic shades of black, white, silver, and gray, enriching his tonal scheme only slightly in the central mazurka episode, giving the work a ruggedness that has none of the richness or warmth of its C minor predecessor.

The work opens softly with ominous rumbles in the bass that grow louder, quickly swelling into a hurricane. There is a dramatic pause before the serpentine main melody enters (0:18), proud and fierce yet unmistakably tragic in character, impelled forward by snarling trills over a savage polonaise rhythm. This long melody, which makes explicit the hazy melodic profile of the introduction, is built of a chain of individual components. The second of these is a doleful tune that emerges in the right hand (0:36) over the main theme, which is now stated in the bass, followed by another series of drum-roll-like trills down below, then an element in a cantering rhythm (0:46), and then (0:55) a series of thundering chords and trills that form the tail of the first group.

At 1:00 there is an abrupt change of key to a faraway B-flat minor, and the second theme—proud and grief-stricken, and perhaps just a bit feminine compared to the macho primary sequence—appears. The main theme returns (1:20), now rendered with cataclysmic power, followed by the complementary tune (1:38), the cantering element (1:48), and the second theme (2:03). The main theme is reiterated, with runs in the left hand adding yet more ferocity and impetus. But at 3:08 a series of chords in an easier rhythm that move away from the relentless minor-key tonalities of the opening section suggest that a change is at hand.

Now (3:19) something startling occurs. A powerful rhythmic sequence—beginning with a hard single note (A) followed by a quickly spinning figure followed by three more brusque notes, another spinning group, and finally four sharply accented notes—replaces the tragic melody of the polonaise. As smart pianists have long recognized and taken pains to clarify in performance (and as Charles Rosen has shown in his book *The Romantic Generation*), Chopin here imitates the sound of drums in the field, with the spinning notes mimicking a snare with uncanny accuracy, and the other notes a bass drum. Throughout this long sequence, which lasts for nearly two minutes of the work's eleven-minute playing time, Chopin repeats that dry A thirty-five times against shifting harmony in the spinning figure, using repetition to create a tension that is almost unbearable. (Chopin also uses repetition hypnotically but to a very different effect in the Berceuse, op. 57—track 11— a lullaby with ornate variations). This daring episode is the ancestor of Ravel's nerve-wracking Bolero of 1928, probably the most famous musical work in which repetition creates tension. The drum sequence is interrupted but once—and briefly—at 4:07 by the second theme, before it returns, spinning down quietly (5:00), as the mazurka, large in scale and with a heroic feeling like the polonaise that surrounds it, begins at 5:05.

Bringing welcome relief from the savagery of the polonaise and the hair-raising drum episode, the mazurka begins with a gracefully drooping opening theme, including a short, rhythmically hesitating tail that recurs throughout this long section. The second melody, in an irregular rhythm, begins at 5:27, and an upward-reaching motif that is at once nostalgic and epic leads to the reprise of the first tune (5:37). Another high-flown theme appears at 5:59, followed by a more graceful dance that moves downward (6:05), then yet another mazurka theme of a gentler character (6:20). A murmuring left hand leads to an emotional intensification of the opening melody, now rewritten in richer harmonic garb over a surging bass. The first mazurka theme comes back yet again (7:06), in its grandest incarnation, trailed by the other mazurka tunes. But at 8:12, a familiar rumbling in the left hand tells the listener that something is about to change: it is the sullen motif of the introduction, which is about to be fully repeated. There is a sudden, shrill upward run (8:28), a long pause, and then another appearance of the introductory figure, followed by another terrifying run at 8:43.

The storm of octaves that formed the introductory section comes back (8:49), followed by the polonaise itself (9:02) in (to borrow Melville's phrase) "the nameless regal overbearing dignity of some mighty woe." Although—or perhaps because—it is felt as inevitable, the effect of the theme at this moment is overwhelming. The second theme makes its final appearance (9:46), and the main melody is heard again with rushing left-hand runs (10:06). At 10:43 the rhythmic tail of the main thematic group takes on new urgency, as it presses forward into the coda, where Chopin seems to wrestle with overflowing emotions, particularly at 10:55 as chords in the right hand totter above huge trills and a run in the left. The main tune passes into the bass at 10:59, as the sorrowful complementary melody is heard one last time. Finally, echoing and balancing the introduction, the rhythm of the main melody is reduced to its most basic profile (11:12), beneath throbbing chords. There are some final percussive rumbles as this harshest of Chopin's masterpieces ends on terrifying bare octaves.

Chopin's reputation as a "feminine" composer of salon music is particularly baffling once one knows the F-sharp minor Polonaise, a work as brutally masculine, and even barbaric, as anything by composers whose music seems testosterone driven, such as Beethoven or Verdi. And as forbidding it is, the op. 44 Polonaise is a splendid example of how much great music can express at one moment: here is a work on the pages of which sorrow, pride, and wrath mingle freely and with no sense that any of these emotions is out of place. While its musical content is highly dramatic, the work's innovative structure and disdain for small ways allows it to speak in an epic voice. Its most ambitious descendant is the *Polonaise-fantaisie,* op. 61, which, though profoundly beautiful, fails to cohere like the grim, great F-sharp minor Polonaise.

With its glorious, unforgettable main theme and triumphant spirit, the A-flat major Polonaise, op. 53, composed between 1842 and '43, has always been one of Chopin's most popular compositions. It is also one of the great virtuoso showpieces, probably serving as the closing selection on more piano recital programs than any single work. But its popularity has come at the cost of trivialization, by a public that has grown familiar with its manifold beauties and in innumerable distorted performances by pianists eager to show off their virtuoso chops. The tempo indication for the A-flat Polonaise, like that of the E-flat minor, is *maestoso* (majestic), which calls for a deliberate pace, but hectic performances have been the rule since its publication. Chopin's friend and admirer Charles Hallé reported that the composer complained about "how unhappy he felt because he had heard his *Grande Polonaise* in A-flat *jouée vite!* [played fast], thereby destroying all the grandeur, the majesty, of this noble inspiration." Performances that are too fast and too loud are still common enough. The A-flat Polonaise is an intricate, thematically complex work, into which Chopin also wrote much subtle variation of tempo and dynamics.

It begins with an exciting introduction that anticipates much of what will follow. There are, for example, two figures in the bass that clearly foreshadow a famous passage later in which the sound of charging cavalry is evoked. When the famous main theme enters, many pianists play it at full volume, although Chopin carefully marked it to be played *forte* (loud), in anticipation of its second appearance, where is to be played *fortissimo* and to overwhelming effect. As in many of the polonaises, the melody ends in a tail replete with trills. The rushing brilliance of a scale leads to a repeat of the triumphant melody, now revealed, *fortissimo,* in all of its splendor.

A second theme in F minor is prepared for by a sharply accented transitional passage, before the main theme returns. Then, introduced by a sequence of mighty arpeggiated chords, the cavalry charge begins. This thrilling tone painting of horses' hoofbeats never lapses into banality, thanks to Chopin's unfailing taste. It is supposed to begin softly and then build very gradually in volume, but plenty of pianists ignore Chopin's dynamic marking and thunder away from the start, or start softly and then raise the volume before they should. The stunning episode is followed by a passage where Chopin, a master of pacing, cools things down, giving the listener and pianist a minute to relax with a quieter passage, mostly in F minor. This builds toward the final iteration of the main theme and a push toward the magnificent coda, which ends the work in a thunderous statement of the polonaise rhythm.

Chopin's final essay in the form is the *Polonaise-fantaisie* in A-flat major, op. 61, composed in 1846. While this very late work is undoubtedly a masterpiece, Chopin struggles to find the proper form for the musical and emotional depths it plumbs. The work baffled performers and audiences until the middle of the twentieth century, when pianist Vladimir Horowitz took up its cause; today it is one of the most frequently played of the polonaises. It is in the Chopin repertory of every pianist with aspirations to serious musicianship.

Characterized by rapid changes of mood and harmony and a profound unease, this tone poem on Poland's lost greatness begins with a two-chord motif built on an unexpected harmonic shift, followed by a rainbow of arching tones. Chopin's tempo marking is the familiar *allegro maestoso.* The opening sequence is repeated four times, creating a bardic atmosphere, as though the listener is hearing the recounting of an ancient legend. A ruminative episode throws out melodic fragments while laying out the harmonic profile of much that will follow. The polonaise rhythm is stated alone in the right hand, and the main melody, songful and soulful, is heard. An agitated passage leads to a fierce climax, followed by a chromatic avalanche and then a more playful rendition of the opening. The polonaise rhythm is repeated obsessively throughout. The main theme returns in a passionate incarnation over a rippling bass, leading to another febrile outburst. Then follows another lull, after which Chopin renders the melody in his most lavish operatic style.

There is one more dramatic outburst, in B major and marked *piu lento* (more slowly), before the middle section begins. This dreamlike sequence, with its moving melody and fabulously rich harmonic movement, is the still center of the work, reaching its climax, perhaps Chopin's most inward looking, on a series of mystical trills reminiscent of Beethoven's late piano works. These prepare the way for a return of the opening legendary passage, now rendered softly and back in A-flat, which could not sound more dreamily remote from the B major tonality in which the listener's ear has been saturated. The right hand picks up an impassioned phrase from the middle section, leading to a passage of mounting excitement and a thunderous climax of Wagnerian intensity. There is a sudden, shattering change of key to B major and then an equally shocking return to A-flat, as the feverish vision of Polish horsemen galloping triumphantly into the distance disappears. The uproar of the final apotheosis is impressively orchestral in effect, but the glorious central section, perhaps Chopin's most spiritual passage, is always hard to follow.

The rapid changes of mood and texture in the *Polonaise-fantaisie* make it the most difficult of Chopin's large-scale works to put across in performance, requiring a virtuoso of uncommon sensitivity. It needs to be played with passionate conviction and an eye always on the long thematic line. Great performances of the work are rare, but in the right hands, it can be unbearably moving.

The Individual Works

Although Chopin returned again and again to the waltz, mazurka, polonaise, impromptu, scherzo, and ballade, his output contains a fair number of one-offs as well. Apart from their increasing greatness as the date of composition and opus numbers rise, there is no thread of individual development that unifies or animates them. Two early works, the Rondo in C minor, op. 1, and the *Variations brillante,* op. 12, are never played. There is the pleasant but inconsequential Introduction and Rondo, op. 16, and the uneasy mix of ideas that is the Bolero, op. 19. The Tarantelle, op. 43, is certainly polished but seems lifeless. But the Fantasy in F minor, op. 49; the Berceuse (the French word meaning lullaby), op. 57; and the Barcarolle, op. 60, date from Chopin's peak years and rank among the finest manifestations of his mature style.

Unlike the *Andante spianato* and *Grande polonaise brillante,* the Introduction and Rondo, op. 16, was written as a single, inseparable piece. True salon music, the work is light but charming and very difficult to play. It is rarely performed, apart from Vladimir Horowitz's attempt to revive it in a brilliant 1971 recording that gained no traction but is well worth hearing nonetheless. The Introduction, which begins in a melancholy C minor, is lovely, while the cheerful and energetic Rondo, in E-flat, burbles along in dizzying whirls of ornamentation similar in profile to that of the contemporaneous Etude in G-flat major, op. 10, no. 5 (the "Black Key") but with less steel in its spine.

The Bolero is perhaps the most formally clumsy work by this polished composer: a disjointed thing that begins with a long introduction, followed by a fretful tune of vaguely Spanish flavor set over the familiar polonaise rhythm, and then by a melody that sounds a lot like the main theme of the A major Polonaise, op. 40, no. 1, but with none of that work's élan. It is touching to know that our hero was mortal after all. The Tarantelle, op. 43, of 1841, presents a more complex puzzle. Apparently composed during a fad in Paris for this Neapolitan dance, Chopin's displays all the technical finish one would expect of a work of its relatively late date and high opus number, with little in the way of his usual passion or profundity. But the Tarantelle's slippery harmonic movement and technical difficulty make the work worth listening to, and it would make an interesting and effective encore in an all-Chopin recital.

The *Allegro de concert,* op. 46, is the least known of Chopin's significant individual works and one of the largest in scale. This elaborate fourteen-minute composition on which Chopin labored from the mid-1830s until 1841 is apparently the opening movement of an uncompleted third piano concerto in A major. Orchestral and solo entrances will be easily identifiable to listeners with a few concertos from the classical era under their belts. This sense of not entirely comfortable adaptation from concerted piece to solo renders the *Allegro de concert* awkward and undesirable for pianists as a recital piece, particularly with so many formal masterpieces by Chopin to choose from. (The *Grande polonaise brillante,* op. 22, with its smaller orchestral part, makes the transition far more gracefully).

But the *Allegro de concert* is worth hearing for the very beautiful material of which it is built. The quiet opening in march rhythm has considerable melodic and harmonic subtlety; the second theme is a vast melody of a rare and exotic gorgeousness. What would have been the entrance of the soloist is a magnificent and elaborate flourish for the right hand leading to one of Chopin's uncanny re-imaginings of a Bellinian melody, followed by a swirling figure much like those that conclude the thematic groups in the first movements of the two completed concertos. There is not much in the way of development of these themes, which are restated with difficult ornamental passagework before being brought to an end with a thunderous reiteration of the opening tune. Although the *Allegro de concert* may be Chopin's most ungainly child, he was justified in not wanting to dispose of a work made of such marvelous material. Perhaps this master manipulator of form gave up on finding another outlet for his fine ideas before finally sending them into the world in this imperfect shape.

The F minor Fantasy of 1841 is one of Chopin's largest and most important compositions. In this gravely beautiful work, Chopin experiments on a large scale with keys, using the F minor of the opening section interchangeably with its very close relative A-flat major and in turn playing these off the middle section's remote B major, as he would later repeat to even more telling effect in the *Polonaise-fantaisie*. Reflecting his obsession at that period with funeral marches—consider the C minor Prelude from op. 28, the third movement of the op. 35 Sonata, and the Nocturnes in C minor of op. 48 and F minor of op. 55—Chopin begins this fantasy with a heavy-footed procession that switches regularly and without effort between F minor and A-flat major. The march ends in a more freely moving section that wanders between various keys with the feeling of an awakening after the steady, somber tread of the opening.

Events begin to move more quickly, leading to a turbulent melody in F minor and another easy switch into A-flat for what is one of Chopin's most rapturous melodies, a soaring tune that is like a fragment from an idealized operatic duet. This leads to another stormy transitional section, which is reminiscent of the climax of the first movement of the B-flat minor Sonata but, unlike that passage, merely dramatic rather than terrifying. A fierce chord sequence leads into another march, this one in a triumphant and serene A-flat major. Another agitated passage precedes a repeat of the stormy tune and the celestial melody, but instead of the A-flat march, a dreamlike sequence leads to the middle section, much slower and in B major. Profoundly restful in the midst of the ceremonies and ecstasies of the Fantasy, this brief interlude looks ahead to the parallel passage in the *Polonaise-fantaisie* in the same key, although this section is more chordal and static. At a shift in harmony, the listener is plunged back into the turmoil—with everything but the opening funeral march fully repeated—leading to a huge climax, followed by a moment of exquisite reflection before the serene close in A-flat major.

With its epic scale, direct and sincere expressive posture, glorious thematic material, and potent exploitation of harmony, the Fantasy in F minor is unquestionably one of Chopin's masterworks. It seems less happy structurally, however, than other works of comparable dimension, such as the continuously evolving forms of the F-sharp minor Polonaise and the Barcarolle; or the ballades and scherzos, where themes are developed rather than simply repeated as they are in op. 49. Conceived in large sections, the Fantasy is therefore episodic, with its seams tending to show a bit after repeated listening. It is nevertheless a work of undeniable power and beauty that is also exciting and effective in performance.

Composed in 1844, the Berceuse, op. 57 (track 11 on the CD), is a set of fourteen variations on a lullaby—a bare description giving no sense of the witchery of this extraordinary work. Narrowness of focus is what this is about: the theme and variations are all of exactly equal length; the key stays in D-flat major for almost the entire duration; throughout the piece, the left hand plays a rocking accompaniment that changes only minimally; the volume remains soft and the moderate tempo never shifts, except for one minute adjustment toward the end. All the action in the Berceuse takes place in the right hand, which puts the gentle theme through alterations that are as elaborate and brilliant—but always delicate—as imaginable; in spite of what looks on paper like sheer monotony in the left hand set against almost bizarrely frenetic activity in the right, the full effect of the work is profoundly tranquil.

A D-flat major chord broken into a rocking rhythm opens the Berceuse quietly in the left hand, with the vocally styled melody entering softly in the right at 0:08. A second voice, creating the first variation, enters below the melody (0:21). In the second variation (0:36), the second voice moves in a different direction and then in a slightly different rhythm from the melody, which still floats above. The tune is rendered in grace notes over an unchanging A-flat in the third variation (0:52), first among the bejeweled incarnations of the theme, which has traveled far from the vocally inspired theme into the realm of pure piano sound.

Variation 4 opens with a trill, followed by the theme broken into rapid notes; the next (1:20) presents the theme in a new rhythm that makes it shimmer like sunshine on water. The sixth variant, beginning at 1:36, breaks the theme into glistening fragments, while the seventh (1:51) presents the melody in close, difficult descending figuration. No. 8 (2:06) breaks the theme into lovely chords high on the keyboard, followed by arabesques. The ninth variation (2:23) is all fast-moving decoration in quick little notes, while the tenth (2:38) is full of runs and trills, as though a nightingale has picked up the song from the garden outside the nursery window.

With the eleventh (2:58), we return to a simpler, more vocal presentation, as Chopin asks that the tempo be slowed just a bit, creating the sense that the work is moving gently toward its end. So delicate is the aural surface that the slightest change, like this one, makes a big impression. Twelve (3:13) is again slightly more pianistic. With the thirteenth variation (3:30) comes a destabilizing note that represents the first and only change in harmony, making another major impact on the fine-boned texture of the Berceuse as the key moves to G-flat major; the last variation seems a long-breathed continuation of its predecessor. At 3:58 the theme returns—back in the D-flat major tonality to which Chopin has held so stubbornly, except for the last two variations, over the course of four-and-a-half minutes—as the piece seems to close its eyes rather than end.

In the Berceuse, Chopin uses rare art to hypnotize his audience: it is a shame to have to pick apart a work so delicate and enchanting. But is worth noting that the elaborate decorations in which the beautiful little theme is draped introduce countless changes to its rhythmic profile and harmony. The ear is tickled by the slight tartness of all those tiny notes outside of D-flat major that swarm so busily around the theme, which seems at times ready to break up in figuration, but of course the steady flow of the rocking left hand holds everything together. The Berceuse is also a prime example of Chopin's supreme mastery of piano technique and sound: only a composer with an absolute understanding of the instrument's expressive capabilities could have dreamed it up.

Chopin's love of Italian melody and modernist inclinations come together triumphantly in the Barcarolle, op. 60, written between 1845 and '46. One of his supreme achievements, the Barcarolle is loved by audiences for its sensuous beauty and revered by composers—including Brahms, Fauré, Debussy, and Ravel—for the immense sophistication of its compositional technique. Under the direct influence of Chopin, Fauré composed thirteen works of the same title over the course of his career. Ever-changing, hazy harmonies like those heard in the Barcarolle can be found throughout Debussy's oeuvre—for example, in the two books of preludes for piano, the Violin Sonata, *L'isle joyeuse,* and the *Prélude á L'après-midi d'une faune.* One of Debussy's students attested to that master's particular admiration for the work, writing that "the way in which he analyzed and explained this piece was something special." Ravel put himself on record about the Barcarolle, commenting that it "sums up the sumptuously expressive art of this great Slav of Italian education.... In it Chopin made real all that his predecessors managed to express only imperfectly." Its structure, like that of the F-sharp minor Polonaise, is in three broad sections, but subdivided into smaller groups that give the piece its own logic and a powerful sense of rise and fall and of forward movement, albeit at a less driven pace than that of the Polonaise. The work is also interesting for bearing the weight of a dramatic scenario—the unmistakable impression that it tells a story, like many of the nocturnes, its closest relatives in the composer's output.

This apotheosis of the Venetian gondolier's song opens with a booming note in the bass, followed by a floating, flowing group; there is a pause, and then the rocking figure that runs through much of it begins softly in the left hand. But the opening sequence already shows itself to be of the utmost interest and importance. On the narrative level, one can easily picture, in the words of writer Jeremy Siepmann, "the decisive push of the gondolier's pole and the swish of the water as he launches the boat on its journey." It is hard to imagine much of Debussy's music without the territory blazed by this passage alone. After a statement of the serene rocking rhythm that dominates the work, the long, ripe melody appears, two notes at a time, suggesting that, like the D-flat Nocturne, this is a duet. *Italianissimo* but popular rather than operatic in character, Chopin marks it to be played *cantabile* (songfully). One right-hand motif suggests the glinting of light on the water; another the slapping of water against the side of the boat; a third looks directly back at the sliding melodic figure that is the main theme of the G major Nocturne, op. 37, no. 2, a barcarolle in all but name and the closest relative in Chopin's output to op. 60. The melody returns, heavily decorated with shuddering trills that sound sensuous, perhaps even erotic, as a climax seems to approach but is broken off.

The middle section, in the distant key of A major, is built on a restrained, almost inward melody that will reappear to great effect in the long coda above a rocking motion in the left hand; this section builds with extraordinary rhythmic and harmonic intensity before the introduction of another sweet but fervent melody (again, more like popular song than operatic aria) that will return as the climax; as in the F minor Ballade, what turns out to be the climactic melody enters modestly in the guise of a secondary theme. Here, however, it breaks off in another rocking passage with a temporizing quality, similar to the second theme of the G major Nocturne. This is followed by one of Chopin's greatest inspirations, a voluptuous phrase in which some claim to discern a kiss between the lovers in the gondola, an unusually specific impression that for once does not seem farfetched. Chopin's instruction to the player at this critical point is *dolce sfogato,* meaning sweetly exhaled or unloosed: highly unusual in an instrumental work. The direction has nothing to do with heavy breathing, though; its purpose is to let the player know that the passage is to be phrased vocally, as though delicately sung. The intertwined melodic lines that follow do, however, continue to suggest a tender dialogue. The first theme returns, building to a thickly scored climax on the sweet melody introduced in the middle section. Then one of Chopin's most extended codas begins, using the falling figure that was first introduced in the middle section, which is now made to soar above and cut through the hazy harmonic atmosphere.

This great passage, all twilit glory and vast in scale, looks back to the dying-fall codas of many of the nocturnes, although it far exceeds even the longest of these in length and scope. It clearly inspired Brahms, whose Piano Sonata no. 2 of 1852 ends in a passage not at all coincidentally in the same key; replete with the same kinds of long runs, it is a direct and obvious tribute to and descendent of the conclusion of the Barcarolle.

Chopin wrote other works as great as the Barcarolle but none that surpass it. This opulent music has everything: richly sensuous tunes, rhythmic drive, harmonic sophistication, and a bold new form that springs directly and naturally from the material. It also proffers a penetrating and enveloping sensuality that is nearly shocking. Like much of Chopin's music, its beauty speaks clearly to the musically uninitiated, while there is also more than enough richness and complexity to satisfy the most jaded ear.

A complete recording of his music—like Idil Biret's, from which the selections on the accompanying CD were taken—reveals why Chopin's batting average is so high: he was an acute self-critic, who let only his best efforts see the light of day. Apart from the notable exceptions of the Mazurkas of opp. 67 and 68 and the Waltzes of opp. 69 and 70, the music Chopin chose not to publish is a bit weaker than the canonic works. Among the dozens of Chopin's works, large and small in scale, that can be called masterpieces are some of surpassing greatness. The Barcarolle, one of the landmarks of nineteenth-century music and a signpost for that of the twentieth, stands among them.

Lyricism and Drama in Fixed Forms
The Impromptus and Scherzos

hopin composed four impromptus and four scherzos that share a three-part form but differ radically in content and scale. Nor do the names reflect the nature of the works accurately: the impromptus are longish, highly finished lyrical structures, far from the improvisations the title suggests, while the scherzos (meaning "jokes" in Italian) are large-scale dramatic—and often grim—masterworks. The scherzos are correctly revered and heard often, but as a group, the impromptus are undervalued and neglected. It may be that the relatively restrained emotions and stylized expression of the impromptus work against them with audiences accustomed to Chopin's more passionate utterances, a loss for listeners and performers alike. Except for moving at quicker tempos, these fine pieces bear fairly close melodic and formal resemblance to some of the nocturnes. They are without exception works of charm and beauty that deserve to be better known; at least one—the second, op. 36—is of considerable stature.

Schubert wrote eight masterful, well-known impromptus that, like Chopin's, are major works on which the composer clearly labored long and hard. Schumann's *Impromptus on a Theme of Clara Wieck*, op. 5, is a set of twelve variations on a short theme by his wife, who was one of the most famous pianists of the era. It too is elaborately conceived, and it takes eighteen minutes to play; different in form from Chopin's impromptus and most of Schubert's, there is in Schumann's work no sense of free improvisation either. The title therefore seems to have suggested to composers of the era little more than an instrumental work of basically lyrical character.

Chopin's four impromptus all follow a three-part form (handily referred to by musical scholars as ABA) in which the opening and closing sections are built of the same material, usually busy with figuration, while the middle section consists of a contrasting idea, generally a memorable melody. (The F-sharp major Impromptu presents the outstanding exception in the group to the standard format.) Some of Schubert's impromptus, composed in 1827 and therefore predating Chopin's, have a three-part structure, but not all: the B-flat major, D. 935, no. 3, is a theme and variations, while the great G-flat major, D. 899, no. 3, presents two complementary themes of profoundly lyrical cast over a rippling accompaniment that unifies them into a gripping whole.

The date of composition of the first Impromptu in A-flat major, op. 29, is uncertain, but scholars suggest about 1837. Once the second-most popular impromptu after the *Fantaisie-impromptu*, the work is little heard nowadays—a shame, because it is beautiful, with a lovely, open keyboard texture. It begins with a fast, fluid, almost loopy melody that also carries an anxious edge reminiscent of some of Schumann's contemporaneous masterpieces for piano (listen to *Traumes-Wirren*, the seventh of his Fantasy Pieces, op. 12). The middle section is built around a noble, long-spanned operatic melody in F minor that contrasts vividly with the nervous whirls of the opening. This dissolves into a series of trills that precedes the return of the opening melody, which is replayed in full. A brief, unexpected pause introduces the coda: an effective sequence of a whirling figure alternating with calm chords, the chords winning out quietly in the end.

The greatest of the impromptus is surely the second, in F-sharp major, op. 36, a product of 1839. With a noticeable expansion of form and more powerful content than its companions, the work is boldly experimental but inexplicably neglected, and therefore perhaps more deserving of reconsideration and rehabilitation than any of Chopin's works. The three-part form is here stretched considerably by the addition of transitional material that carries important structural functions, and Chopin reverses the standard order of the material, opening with a songful subject and placing the sharper, more aggressive theme second. There are also several startling changes of key and one of the most brilliantly decorated melodic passages in Chopin's very ornamented output.

Reminiscent of one of the big nocturnes of the same period, the F-sharp major Impromptu opens softly in the left hand with the accompanying figure of steady chords played in a moderate tempo and even pulse. There are also several anticipations of the Barcarolle—notably in the use of the same key and the gentle boom of the opening note, followed by the regular accompanying figure in the left hand, here taking its time over the course of an unusual six-bar phrase. The songful melody enters, dreamlike in a placid descending phrase that soon takes some interesting harmonic turns and is subjected to lavish bel canto decoration. A series of beautiful and tranquil chords marks the end of the opening thematic group while looking ahead to the more forceful rhythmic profile of the middle section; this transitional passage has its own material that will return to marvelous effect as the coda.

The middle section begins quietly, with no change of tempo, but a swing from the soft and hazy F-sharp major to D major, and a dramatic mood shift to a murmuring march rhythm under a melody that can be heard as visionary or nightmarish. This builds quickly to a climax in massive chords over the now thundering march in the bass. The conclusion of this alarming episode and the return of the opening melody are heralded by a short transition of surpassing strangeness, in which Chopin swiftly travels the long harmonic distance between D major and F major, putting the music in one of the most remote keys from the home base of F-sharp major. The opening melody returns over a flowing accompaniment that displaces the original rhythm of the theme, as Chopin moves effortlessly back to the original key, with the melody varied in a faster-moving incarnation. He now speeds up the flow into fast little notes that carry the tune embedded within the ornamentation, as Beethoven often does in his late piano music (listen to the Sonatas opp. 109 and 111 or the Diabelli Variations) or as Chopin himself would again later in the Berceuse and the Barcarolle. The left hand hurries along, carrying the harmony, as the right hand's musical line seems ready to break apart from the sheer lavishness of figuration.

There is a pause before the calm chord sequence that ended the opening thematic group returns, as this fantastical work ends on the rich sonority of a firmly struck F-sharp major chord.

Deploying the lessons learned in writing the first two Impromptus, Chopin composed no. 3 in G-flat major, op. 51, in 1842. The most elegant and urbane of these works, it is also the least played. If not quite on the heroic scale of its predecessor, it is generously proportioned, complex, and satisfying to hear. The work begins with an uncoiling melody, reminiscent of the first theme of the Impromptu no. 1, but in a slightly different dancelike rhythm that gives the tune more room to breathe and with less of the hurried, anxious feeling that pervades op. 29. On its first repetition, the opening melody is harmonized mellifluously. At the end of the first group, Chopin presents the material that will end the work, including a brief series of chords followed by a wistful, rising phrase. A melodic descent led by the left hand leads artfully to the middle section, which consists of another noble tune modeled on the range and sonority of the cello, as the right hand provides the accompaniment with a broken figure. The first group returns, and the work ends with the chords and the rising phrase in a grand and graceful gesture.

The *Fantaisie-impromptu* in C-sharp minor, op. 66, once one of Chopin's best loved works, has fallen on hard times. Chopin chose not to publish the piece, which he composed in the mid-1830s—surely a telling decision for this proud self-critic, although there are accounts by his pupils of his having taught it. The work was edited and published in 1855 by his pupil and friend Jules Fontana, who for reasons of his own added "fantaisie" to the composer's straightforward title. It quickly achieved phenomenal popularity, with the melody of the middle section being appropriated for use in the 1917 popular song "I'm Always Chasing Rainbows," which is listed as having words by Joseph McCarthy and music by Harry Carroll! (Carroll adapted Chopin's melody to the song format.) The mid-twentieth-century barber-turned-crooner Perry Como had a hit with it in 1945, again demonstrating how profoundly vocal were Chopin's inspiration for and the shaping of his great melody.

With its simple form and light textures, the *Fantaisie-impromptu* was bound for a fall as it was measured over the decades for a more accurate estimation of its place in Chopin's output—which is not to suggest that the work lacks merit. It contains two highly memorable melodies—"I'm Always Chasing Rainbows" is one—and the opening and closing sections present a rhythmic difficulty that requires a very solid technique, if not virtuosity at the highest level. Now outranked by so many of Chopin's masterworks, the once ubiquitous *Fantaisie-impromptu* is performed only rarely.

It begins with a brief but arresting statement in the left hand leading immediately into a sweeping Alberti bass figure. The first theme, breathless and in a different rhythmic pattern than the bass, enters quickly, soon sprouting a second melody with a pleading quality. The tempo broadens; the left hand slows, as the familiar, magnificently operatic tune ("I'm Always Chasing Rainbows") of the central episode is spun out in leisurely fashion. The return of the opening section is at a quicker pace and in a more urgent tone, but Chopin has a trick up his sleeve: the great tune from the middle, here recited by the left hand beneath an obsessive spinning figure in the right, as the piece runs down to a hushed and dreamlike conclusion. Chopin obviously had his reasons for withholding the C-sharp minor Impromptu from publication, but there is nothing to apologize for here.

Scherzos began to appear as individual movements in instrumental works in the early eighteenth century. Bach's Keyboard Partita no. 3 in A minor contains one: a short, light dance in a brisk rhythm that bears no relation to Chopin's enormous creations. Haydn used the title on several occasions, but these are uniform neither in form nor rhythm. The most notable of Haydn's scherzos—a minuet in all but name—serves as second movement of the String Quartet in G major, op. 33, no. 5, published in 1782.

It was Beethoven who breathed life into the scherzo, using it in place of the minuet as the third movement (occasionally the second) of his instrumental compositions as early as 1795: the first Piano Sonata (op. 2, no. 1) contains a minuet but the second (op. 2, no. 2) a scherzo.

Beethoven's Symphony no. 1 has a minuet that is really a scherzo, while the third movement of the Second Symphony, accorded the title of scherzo, is of considerable dimension and energy. Beethoven composed many great scherzo movements over the course of his career, perhaps the most famous being the titanic one in the Ninth Symphony, but all share an emphatic rhythmic profile that reveals the form's descent from dance, and a three-part structure in which the opening and closing sections are of the same material, with a contrasting middle part (ABA).

While there is naturally considerable variation in scope and tone among Beethoven's many scherzos, most, like Chopin's, display a rough energy that often turns boisterous, more than occasionally exploding into violence. Unlike Chopin, though, Beethoven never viewed the scherzo as an independent piece; all stand as movements within larger works. And while Chopin's four independent scherzos may have Beethoven's basic form and character, with perhaps one exception they sound nothing like Beethoven. They are four of Chopin's most characterful and distinctive works, each quite different from the others. All are in triple time, but unlike Beethoven's, they have virtually no inherited sense of the dance. What is unprecedented in Chopin's four scherzos are their formal scope, which is large in the earliest and grows in each succeeding piece, and their dramatic intensity. Apart from the extraordinary exception of no. 4, they express conflict; all four grip the listener with their unflagging force from beginning to end.

Mendelssohn composed a number of scherzos as well, including the very great one for orchestra in his incidental music to *A Midsummer Night's Dream,* but they are "fairy music," lighter in texture and mood than Beethoven's or Chopin's, as is the Queen Mab Scherzo from Berlioz's *Roméo et Juliette.* The "sonata form" composers who came after Beethoven, from Schubert through Mahler, largely followed that master's lead when writing scherzo movements for their instrumental works. A young Brahms wrote a burly Scherzo in E-flat minor in 1851, modeled on Chopin's works (particularly the Scherzo no. 2) but with two contrasting middle sections instead of one. Apart from several highly interesting exceptions, notably the third movement of his Symphony no. 3, Brahms's scherzos are clearly from the Beethoven mold.

Some uncertainty surrounds the date of composition of the Scherzo no. 1 in B minor, op. 20. Originally thought to be the product of 1831 to '32, this dark and powerful piece is now assigned to 1834 or '35, the latter being the year of its publication. While Chopin wrote some great music during the earlier years, all of it is in shorter forms: the B minor Scherzo is likely the earliest of Chopin's masterworks on a large scale, with the possible exception of the contemporaneous Ballade no. 1, op. 23. The thematic material of the first and third sections of this powerful triptych is based completely on the resources of the piano: this is no takeoff on Italian opera, nor could any other single instrument deploy the combination of power and flexibility Chopin musters from the keyboard here, from roaring chords to fast-moving passagework. The B minor Scherzo may be Chopin's earliest masterwork, and it is certainly one of his gloomiest. Technically difficult, it can be thrilling in the hands of a virtuoso, but the most brilliant performance cannot soften the very rough edges of this powerful expression of anxiety and rage.

With an opening thematic group comprised of fragments, the first Scherzo sets the pattern for all four. Two crashing, dissonant chords start the work, the first a shriek in the upper register, the second a grim reply wrenched from the guts of the piano, plunging the listener immediately into an atmosphere of turbulence and terror. The chords have a function that is structural and not merely introductory; they will recur later in the work. The next theme enters, boiling furiously, with a melody emerging from the figuration like bubbles that rise and burst on its surface. Chopin would use the same kind of writing to entirely different effect in a number of other works, including the sunny scherzo that is the second movement of the Sonata in B minor, op. 58, of 1844; later composers, notably Debussy and Ravel, would learn much from this method. This is hardly a conventional tune but rather a series of notes, skimming along like fragments atop the swarming activity of both hands below, which often seems ready to spin out of control.

Like everything in this headlong tragedy, the contrasting second group arrives quickly, in the shape of brooding, grandly expressive chords that do not, however, long slow the impetuous flow of the opening sequence. Another incarnation of the seething opening carries on its surface another sighing melodic fragment, less a melody than the ghost of one. This too is overwhelmed by the furious tide of figuration that leads ultimately back to the main theme. The sweeping chord sequence prepares the way for the middle section, in a gentle B major and at a much slower speed, a moment of peace in this otherwise comfortless sea. Nothing could be more welcome to the listener's frayed ears and nerves.

A delicate melody apparently drawn from a Polish Christmas carol floats above a gently rocking accompaniment. The tune grows eloquent as it widens in range, but the overall effect of the central panel is hypnotic and soothing. A minute shift in harmony signals trouble, though, as the chords that opened the piece harshly break in, plunging the listener back into the turmoil of the first thematic group. The expressive chords that form the second theme prepare the way for the coda—a brilliant sequence of rushing figures interrupted by a massive, dissonant chord, hammered ten times with the utmost ferocity—before a furious, boiling passage and a rushing scale seem to fling the music to its shattering conclusion.

Long the best known and most popular of the scherzos, no. 2 in B-flat minor, op. 31 (composed in 1837), balances the form's familiar drama and virtuosity with a magnificent lyrical counterweight. As the British musicologist and Chopin scholar Jim Samson has pointed out, Chopin also experiments with the basic three-part form in both this scherzo and the third, blurring the lines between the sections, playing themes off each other, and developing them over the length of the works. Finally, in this work, as in the Fantasy in F minor, Chopin uses two keys (B-flat minor and D-flat major) interchangeably, allowing him to jump abruptly between dramatic and lyrical elements. This work is a good example of Chopin's gift at writing music that stirs the emotions of the listener while challenging and satisfying the mind at the same time.

The work opens unambiguously in B-flat minor with an urgent, whispered question couched in a rumbling, rhythmic motif, followed by a strikingly long pause and then a reply in crashing chords. The long, silent pauses between the various thematic elements as they are presented and played out are among the most remarkable features of this great work, the dramatic silences filling the role of lead actors in the drama no less than the played notes. They are crucial not only to the scherzo's musical fabric but to its effective performance as well: woe to the pianist who fails to observe their full duration and make sure that the silences are absolute, with no sound coming from the piano. Without this, the scherzo loses much of its dramatic power, while on the other hand, scrupulous observance of the silences guarantees a more effective performance.

The "question" motif, silences, and crashing chords are repeated a number of times, after which very high and low notes, sounded simultaneously, mark the change of key to D-flat major and the appearance of the lyrical theme, another of Chopin's soaring operatic gems over a swiftly flowing Alberti bass figure. This great melody is played out at length, as it moves into a more rhythmically aggressive ending in richly harmonized chords, leading to a fantastic bouncing figure that brings the opening group to an end firmly in D-flat major.

So many contrasting ideas have been presented in less than a minute that a good performance of this scherzo will already have the listener breathless: we have heard themes presented in laconic rhythmic form and as passionate, long-spun melody; tensely muttered inquiries and splendid loud chords; high tones juxtaposed against deep ones; the twinned tonalities of B-flat minor and D-flat major. Most startling of all is how Chopin has pitted sound and silence, elementally, against one another.

The middle section, in A major, opens quietly with chords delicately wrapped in *fiorature* (the same kind of flowerings used to decorate melodies in the nocturnes) that look ahead to the third Scherzo. Another, more serious theme is presented, different in melodic shape but reminiscent in rhythm to the questioning phrase that opens and animates the entire work. A light, rushing figure appears in the right hand, and the themes are here combined and worked out in a more dramatic way than in the quiet central part of the B minor Scherzo. The more serious, sharply rhythmed theme dominates these proceedings; the second theme from the opening group, in which very high and low notes are sounded together appears; and it is with a sense of inevitability that, as the violence of this section dies down, the opening motif returns, its way having been prepared by what the ear now recognizes as a variety of familiar material. It is also now clear that Chopin has indeed used sonata technique, combining and developing themes, to make the return of the opening theme sound very much like its *recapitulation*—simply its return in original form after its travels through a development. The opening material is played out, straight through once more, leading to a headlong coda of unbearable excitement and dramatic force, where harmonic jolts are made yet more fierce by sharp rhythmic accentuation as the work ends on a wild reiteration of the high and low notes together. The sense is that the work's potent lyric impulse has triumphed in the end, but only barely.

The C-sharp minor Scherzo, op. 39 (track 12 on the CD)—embodying another wild struggle between lyric and dramatic, with an outcome that seems clearly tragic—was composed in Majorca and Nohant in 1839. In the B-flat minor Scherzo, Chopin is profligate with musical ideas, but the bulk of this work is built of only two themes. This may be the largest of Chopin's structures erected from so little material; the intensity and skill with which they are developed not only precludes any sense of thinness but allows the piece to come across as a particularly stunning feat of composition. These two strongly contrasting musical ideas—the first harsh and angular, the second full and gentle—are thrown into opposition, with explosive results. The C-sharp minor Scherzo also differs from the others in structure: its two main thematic groups alternate but never intersect, and its opening and closing episodes are of entirely different material.

The scherzo opens with one of the most modern passages in nineteenth-century music: a strange, disorienting introduction that is rough going today and must have baffled Chopin's listeners utterly when he first played it. It consists of a slippery rhythm that is not in the clear triple time of the body of the work. There is no melody, just a series of unharmonized notes that sounds as though it could have been lifted from a score by Schoenberg, interspersed with three crashing chords—none of which are C-sharp minor but which, by working around it, do ultimately define the C-sharp minor tonality. Yet this wild curtain raiser sets the tone brilliantly for the distinct personalities of the themes that will follow and for the drama into which they will be plunged.

Nevertheless, the listener is relieved, at least temporarily, to hear the first theme as it pulls into sharp focus at 0:22. Tough and hard-edged and presented in fiercely hammered double octaves, it is difficult to play but exciting to hear, and will provide the strongest possible contrast to the second theme when that appears. But first there is a quiet and glum little tail to the opening episode (0:28), followed by a full repeat of the theme, which is hardly a melody in the conventional sense. At 0:40 the second sequence of the theme appears, another angry tune in a sharp rhythm over a steady but urgent left hand that represents perhaps the closest approach in Chopin's scherzos to the stubborn, driving rhythms of Beethoven's. The theme plays itself out once more, starting in big chords above biting octaves in the left hand (1:01), followed at last by a softening (1:33) that suggests a new idea is coming.

Indeed it is: an astonishing chord sequence (1:37)—with an almost liturgical quality, as well as a reasonably close resemblance to the old tavern hymn "How Dry I Am"—appears gently, followed by a glorious cascade of notes at 1:41 that is one of the most memorable examples in Chopin's output of his matchless ability to exploit the piano's capabilities. Although deliberately not eloquent by Chopin's standards, this second thematic group serves the purpose of providing the strongest possible contrast to the savagery of the first episode. Where that is fast, lean, and angular, this is in slower notes, gentle tone, and rounded edges, always trailed by its breathtaking tail. The soft tune appears—in new harmonies, slightly recast rhythmically, and always followed by its delicate tail—at 1:48 and 1:58. Quiet, simply stated octaves in the bass (2:10) lead to a restatement of the second theme in all its incarnations; at 2:52, the same soft episode in the bass leads to a plume that waves gracefully up instead of down (3:01).

The four phrases of the second theme recur once more at 3:30, this time sounding more serious, as a series of chords (3:58) introduces a more ardent feeling. But an ominous grumbling in the left hand at 4:06 hints at trouble, which does indeed reappear as the upward-moving passage shifts to minor key and the hammering main theme returns in all its ferocity (4:34). The Beethoven-like section returns (4:53), followed once more by the second theme, this time at a slightly slower tempo (5:20). The quiet octave motif recurs (5:51) as prelude to the second theme, now infinitely more expressive in E minor and at an emphatically slower tempo (6:00). At 6:48 Chopin finds a surprising new use for his material in a left-hand sequence that begins quietly, where the second theme's dancing chord sequence acts as a lid holding down the boiling in the left hand. Chopin also builds tension here by holding the harmony rigidly in check to prepare for the scorching coda. That episode, based on new material, begins at 7:17 with a series of biting octaves, followed by blistering passagework. Hammering notes in the left hand below the stinging frenzy of the right (7:26) are followed by a snarling trill (7:36), as the right hand spins above more furious leaps in the left (7:47). At 8:02, the work flings itself to a melodramatic end in a shocking C-sharp major; here, unlike the conclusion of Scherzo no. 2, the sudden introduction of the major key speaks in accents of tragedy and terror.

The C-sharp minor Scherzo is improbably full and thrilling for a large-scale musical work constructed from only two themes. Its effectiveness stems from the radically different character of the two thematic groups, Chopin's skill at varying these subtly, and perhaps most significantly, his artful use of the resources of the piano, from bare, angry octaves to that unforgettable veil of notes in the second subject. At once theatrical, austere, and daring, the C-sharp minor Scherzo is one of Chopin's greatest dramatic inspirations.

The wonderful Scherzo no. 4 in E major, op. 54, composed in 1842 and '43, stands alone among its companion works, and in Chopin's entire output for its mellowness of tone and the deep, Olympian joy it exudes. Like much of Beethoven's late music, it is art that transcends not only the suffering that inevitably attended its creation but the pain of existence itself, with which the chronically ill Chopin was all too familiar. It is the work's radiant spirit that places it among Chopin's most sublime conceptions, although as the best mannered of the scherzos, it is also the most difficult of the four to get to know. After the uproars and rages of the first three, no. 4 can seem low-key to the listener who encounters it for the first time, but for the patient, it will prove an infinitely rewarding companion over the years.

Like its predecessors, the E major Scherzo, the longest by far of the four, opens with an extended thematic group composed of smaller elements. But where Chopin deliberately makes the themes of the earlier works sound disjunctive, here the effect is of great breadth and sweep. The first element is a floating tune that is highly memorable and exceedingly genial, followed by chords in a more accented, dancelike rhythm. A chord sequence flutters up and then down; then a noble phrase in simple octaves, followed by scurrying figuration, makes its appearance. All of these elements have a similar melodic profile, and everything moves at an extremely brisk pace, but the sense of the music is unhurried and exhilarating. The opening section puts the first thematic group through its paces, developing these and taking them abruptly into different keys and back to E major, but always with excellent cheer and an unflagging beauty. There are some moments that parody the drama of the earlier scherzos, particularly some hammered octaves that recall op. 39, but these are pure affect, a dramatic gesture that melts away as they introduce a lilting but earnest phrase leading into the central episode, one of Chopin's most profound and beautiful passages.

The key changes gently to C-sharp minor as the long-spun melody of the middle section enters at a slower tempo. Thoughtful but never melancholy, this splendid tune is heard over a left-hand accompaniment that sounds simple but has an ever-so-slight rhythmic bump that gives it an emotional catch. Both melody and accompaniment are thus provided with room to grow. A second voice enters, enriching the harmony. The atmosphere throughout this entire section is cool and refreshing, as Chopin engages in some of his most refined and delicate tone painting: a bold but effortless shift from C-sharp minor to a distant F major and back again adds to the open, almost outdoor feeling of the music.

The tone of the music intensifies. As the left-hand accompaniment widens in range and length, covering a longer span, the tune broadens as well, building to an emotional climax that is mellow, generous, lordly—there is ecstasy in this music as well. All has been building to the return of the opening theme, which reappears in athletic splendor amid a welter of trills. The entire opening portion is replayed, with even wider harmonic adventuring, adding to the sense of breadth and mobility. The coda, another very long passage, begins with the rhythmic part of the first thematic group tossed gently between the two hands, as an ardent upward run leads into a glorious reiteration of the dancing phrase, a glittering sequence in octaves, and a crystalline E major scale to end this one-of-a-kind masterpiece.

While the stature of the E major Scherzo is unquestioned, it is probably the least performed of the four in recital; each of the other three makes a more exciting and emphatic ending to a program. But the influence, love, and respect op. 54 commands among pianists and composers is considerable. Wagner supposedly disparaged Chopin as a "composer for the right hand," but the titan of German romantic opera learned much from the Polish master. Chopin's bold harmonies predate and specifically anticipate much of what Wagner would later do, of course in a different context. While there is no direct evidence to prove Wagner's knowledge of the E major Scherzo, the musical atmosphere of many passages in acts 1 and 2 of his opera *Siegfried*, composed in 1856 and '57 and set in a forest, suggests it. These are strikingly reminiscent of Chopin's work: harmonically broad and swift, intense and delicate in tone painting, and rich but cool in feeling.

The Mazurkas

E ven in the oeuvre of a composer with a style as distinctive as Chopin's, the mazurkas, which range in playing time from half a minute to a bit over five, stand out for their strong character. In some ways, Chopin never surpassed these fifty-one short dances. The emotions they express range from drunken glee to the deepest sorrow; many are drenched in potent melancholy and longing. But "soulful" is the word that comes to mind again and again when listening to them. Indeed, the composer uses the expression mark *con anima* (with soul) repeatedly throughout. Covering the full range of his maturity—from the exuberant op. 6, written in the early 1830s, to the intimate tragedies of his final years—the mazurkas are Chopin's musical diary, providing our most privileged view into his mind and heart.

Mazurka is actually a generic name covering three types of dances used by Chopin. Differences are subtle, but Chopin's mazurkas can be one or a blend of three distinct folk dances of central Poland: the *mazur,* named for the Polish province of Mazowse, getting top billing but sharing space with the *kujawiak* and—quickest of the three—the *obertas.* Chopin adopts characteristics from all of these, but there appear to be no direct quotations from existing songs and dances in the mazurkas. Instead, Chopin wrote in the style and spirit of the music he had heard as a child, using these rough country dances as points of departure for his infinitely refined and profound tone poems. The mazurkas are not transcriptions or imitations of Polish folk music but rather impressions and recollections transformed into music as art—"classical" music in its highest incarnation.

Chopin knew the dances of the central Polish countryside from an early age, having heard and danced to them at home and on his summer vacations out of Warsaw as a student. Some were performed by a variety of instruments, from a single bagpipe or guitar to small, rustic ensembles of mixed instruments that might include fiddle and double bass, or strings accompanying a bagpipe or shepherd's pipe—or any available combination. Even more primitively, others were simply sung, perhaps when no instruments were available, imparting a completely different character to the dance. Formally, the original dances were typically in two or four parts, but Chopin was flexible in constructing his works. The three-part form (our old friend ABA) predominates, but some mazurkas, like op. 6, no. 4, and op. 7, no. 5, are monothematic, while others (op. 33, no. 4, for example) are multithemed suites of considerable dimension. Many of the earlier mazurkas begin with imposing introductory passages, a practice from which the composer gradually moved away in the later works. Quite a few have long, atmospheric codas, while even more conclude plainly, some to breathtaking effect in midphrase. Throughout the mazurkas, Chopin artfully imitates the sound of instruments, with the drone and squeal of the bagpipe recurring frequently in many works, while others have distinctly vocal-sounding melodies. (Ripe vocal melodies are particularly noticeable in the six mazurkas in A-flat major.) The influence of Italian opera is far less pronounced here than anywhere in Chopin's music but can still be found in some melodic decoration.

Another fingerprint of the mazurka is its curious rhythm, in which the second of the three beats is accented, imparting to the music a hopping feel—unlike the waltz, for example, where the first beat is emphasized. Some (notably the C major, op. 33, no. 3) are quite ambiguous in rhythm, with nothing resembling the pounding patterns of the waltzes or polonaises. This softer, less insistent rhythm lends the mazurkas much of their subtlety and flexibility. But the dances derive their unmistakable sound chiefly from the pungent melodies and harmonies based on those heard in Polish folk music, which stand outside the tonal structures of the classical system. The sound of the intervals inspired by folk music combined with the composer's typical harmonic boldness made the mazurkas tough going for many early listeners.

Chopin composed these at a time when the forebears of the ethnomusicologists of the late nineteenth and early twentieth centuries were beginning to dig for genuine folkloric material. While of course deeply interested in source material himself, Chopin wrote off the work of his contemporary Oskar Kolberg, the first important collector of Polish folk music. But their aims were different: Kolberg's scholarly and omnivorous, Chopin's distillate and artistic. The composer had no forebears in writing these extraordinary evocations of the dance, but there is one direct follower of importance: the Polish composer Karol Szymanowski (1882–1937), whose twenty-two mazurkas in a modern idiom successfully take Chopin's as inspiration and point of departure. They are well worth hearing.

Tchaikovsky inserted a pounding, unsubtle mazurka into act 2, scene 1, of his opera *Eugene Onegin,* and there is a mazurka in form but not name at the end of act 3, scene 1, of Verdi's *Falstaff,* but the great Italian was more interested in what he could do with the hopping rhythm at that point in the action than in copying Chopin's dance. Listeners to the music of Bartók, Scriabin (composer of a number of mazurkas and an early follower of Chopin whose music later took some very strange turns), and Rachmaninoff—not to mention Fauré, Debussy, and Ravel—will feel the influence of Chopin's great dances. Ripples of their expressive intensity, harmonic boldness, and formal compression can perhaps also be sensed in the works of Schoenberg and Webern.

If the Mazurkas from the op. 6 set, composed between 1830 and 1832, are performed relatively infrequently, it is only because there are so many great dances among the remaining forty-seven and not for immaturity or lack of merit. Indeed, they stand with the op. 7 Mazurkas and the three Nocturnes of op. 9 as the first in which Chopin's genius shines in its full glory.

The set begins with a brave work in F-sharp minor, consisting of three dances: the first soulful, the second fiery, and the third playful, ending without bluster in a quiet downward phrase. No. 2, in C-sharp minor, is the first of five in that key, including several of the greatest. This one may not quite be in the exalted company of its fellows from opp. 30, 41, 50, and 63, but it does share with them a hypersensitive emotionality and mysticism that sets the C-sharp minor Mazurkas apart from their peers. Musically, it is also the first mazurka to use the drone bass in imitation of a bagpipe—here at the very beginning, into which an exotic dance theme is embedded to incredible effect. The second theme is granted the expressive marking *gaio* (gaily), otherwise nonexistent in Chopin's output. The drone bass returns once more; the ending of this superb work seems spirited rather than gay.

The latter description applies far better to the next mazurka, the only one of the series in E major. This mock-rustic work also opens with a drone bass onto which Chopin imposes irregular rhythmic accents. There is a grumbling, like that of a double bass, after which the leaping dance tune blazes out in great splendor, but the dance ends demurely. Its joyous descendents include the Mazurkas in B-flat major, op. 7, no. 1, and op. 17, no. 1; in D-flat major, op. 30, no. 3; and B major, op. 63, no. 1. The only mazurka in the somber key of E-flat minor concludes op. 6, a tiny dance—if it can even be regarded as such—reflecting the troubled spirit that animates the Polonaise, op. 26, no. 2, in the same key. Performed at a leisurely tempo, the work takes under forty-five seconds, while swifter ones beat the clock at less than half a minute, but the character of the piece is far from miniature. It is instead fleeting, visionary, unforgettable.

The op. 7 set consists of works composed at the same time as those of op. 6; like that group, it was published in 1832. The first in the set, an ebullient piece in B-flat major, is marked by a bounding melody over a strong bass, in which the accents are placed on the second beat in a manner typical of the form. There is also a fine bagpipe imitation, with a whining tune over a drone bass at its center. An expressive melody over a subdued left hand where notes on the first beat are often omitted marks the opening of the A minor Mazurka, op. 7, no. 2. The middle section in A major is more energetic, but as a whole, the work looks ahead to an entire subspecies of lyrically introspective mazurkas that includes the E minor, op. 17, no. 2; the A minor, op. 59, no. 1; and the F minor, op. 63, no. 2.

The Mazurka in F minor, op. 7, no. 3, is the first of the series that can be called sublime. It begins with a grave, droning introductory passage that is the first imitation in the mazurkas of a guitar—here, it would seem, accompanied by a double bass—followed by an intensely soulful dance melody marked *con anima* over an arpeggiated bass figure in which the first beat is left empty to emphasize the second, as in the previous mazurka. The delicate second theme seems an exquisite extension of the first. The third theme, again over a strumming accompaniment, displays greater rhythmic energy, including the mazurka's characteristic hopping gesture. A new melody appears in the left hand, reinforcing the sense that a double bass was heard in the opening, leading finally into a repeat of that atmospheric passage. The first dance melody is made to reach higher in each of three iterations through the coda, allowing the work to die away to wholly poetic effect as it soars up to a final high note. Because Chopin varies the opening material on its return, the F minor Mazurka is also the first he composed straight through without using repeat marks, which instruct the performer to play a given section again exactly as before. It also looks ahead in form and mood to some of the other big mazurkas, particularly the C-sharp minor, op. 30, no. 4 (track 14 on the CD).

Op. 7 ends with two of the briefest mazurkas in the entire series. No. 4, in A-flat major, consists of a cheerful series of scurrying little dances with a slightly hectic feel—the first and third of which are vocally styled tunes—and a magical, dreamy moment signaled by a sudden and heavy foot on the brakes to accompany a major harmonic shift of great sophistication just before it ends. The fifth of the opus, in C major, is a tiny, monothematic dance that opens with a rhythmic gesture suggesting two hands clapping the time to accompany a merry song danced to a vocal accompaniment, only out in the fields.

With the op. 17 set (1833), the dimensions of the dances begin to expand noticeably, each set climaxing with an extraordinary work. In this opus, as well as the next three, it is the fourth and last mazurka. The B-flat major dance that comes first here, however, is big and bold, opening with a swaggering choreographic gesture and having a comical middle section that sounds like a double bass and squealing shepherd's pipe that can't get their rhythms together. The second dance, in E minor, opens with a sad, expressive melody, but the chromatic rise and fall of the middle section betrays Chopin's immense sophistication. The work ends on a simple but gorgeous fade-out. With the articulate first theme of the A-flat major Mazurka, op. 17, no. 3, the form seems to acquire speech and is so gentle in rhythm that it hardly seems like dance, but the more vehement second theme has a more stamping feel. Certainly the third and fourth themes of this beautiful work are also more choreographic.

Fourth and last in the set, the A minor Mazurka is a leading candidate for the greatest individual work Chopin composed by 1833, a full-fledged masterpiece of the most dreamy, poetic, and melancholy nature. The work opens with gently murmured fragments in the left and then the right hand, followed by the poignant melody, heavily decorated in a manner reminiscent of Chopin's more Italianate works and accompanied by a hesitant left hand. The climax of the melody is a delicate upward gesture of great impact in the restrained and hazy atmosphere of the work. The middle episode in A major moves more steadily but maintains the dreamy atmosphere of the first section, eventually building to a big climax, expressive of terrible longing, that is the only loud moment in the work's otherwise muted dynamic range. The first melody returns, more eloquently decorated. The soft climax is reached one last time as a brooding coda leads to the final phrase, where the fragments that opened the work bring it to a trancelike end.

The first Mazurka of op. 24, composed in 1833, is a slow, sad dance in G minor that opens with a mournful melody, followed by two others that are less overtly somber if hardly cheerful in their own right. The great Mazurka in C major, op. 24, no. 2 (track 13 on the CD), is a good example of Chopin's dance at its most buoyant, also showing his ability to evoke the sounds of a rough country band at the highest artistic level, never letting the music become vulgar or broad. Always moving swiftly, this rustic duet begins softly with a droning figure in both hands, representing the sound of a double bass player drawing a bow across the instrument's strings. The violin player appears in the right hand at 0:04, with a squealing fiddle tune of immense joy and humor. An exuberant stamping figure appears without preparation (0:13), followed at 0:20 by a third tune, in an unprepared move to a third theme in F major that is essentially a variant of the first. This is repeated with subtle, high-flying alterations of its melody at 0:24, 0:29, and 0:33, leading to a return of the first tune at 0:38. The stamping tune follows again (0:47), leading to the central section in D-flat major, one of the most remote keys from C major. Since there is no easy way to bridge this wide tonal chasm, and perhaps emboldened by his earlier successes at jumping between somewhat closer keys, Chopin flexes his knees bravely a few times (0:54) and leaps, landing squarely on the other side and leaving nervous listeners aghast at his recklessness.

The middle section begins with a melody built of the rising and falling of the opening tune combined with the stamping theme, all sounding quite different in D-flat major. These are followed by a droll takeoff on the clumsy double bass player of the opening, who gets his own little solo (1:13) resembling that of the F minor Mazurka op. 7, no. 3, but in an infinitely lighter spirit. This gives Chopin a chance to wander back to C major, which he does by taking a more traditional—if still very short—path, beginning at 1:28. Back now in the home key, the first theme returns for the last time (1:33), followed by the stamping tune (1:42). At 1:50 the opening figure appears—without preparation, like everything else in this astonishing work—fading away now to the fragmented sawing of the bass player, interspersed with long pauses at 1:54, 1:57, and through to the end. Chopin brings this comic masterpiece in at less than two minutes, having achieved everything with wit, delicacy, and breathtaking compositional virtuosity.

The A-flat major Mazurka, which is third in the opus, has an unenviable place between two stunning works, but it is lovely, opening like all the mazurkas in that key with a highly expressive tune. Chopin also emphasizes the high points of the melody with brief but emotional pauses. The middle section consists of a theme that presses ahead more eagerly, while the coda fades away gracefully in the right hand. The B-flat minor Mazurka that closes op. 24 is without question one of the greatest in the series: a remarkable work in which Chopin, as in the E minor Etude, op. 25, no. 5 (track 2 on the CD), employs dissonance to his expressive purpose. In that work, the clashes between notes are tart, but here they are made into something meltingly sweet—or at least, bittersweet. This too is a true keyboard work, hardly imaginable on any other instrument.

A mysterious introduction, in which two lines of notes sidle shyly together from far apart, sets the tone for this dance, in which the melodic lines shift constantly. The rapturous main melody enters in two voices, one slipping upward, the other moving with it at intervals that are dissonant but delicious to the ear; the theme ends in a forceful upward-moving phrase. The main melody lines, woven intimately together as always, reappear in a lower pitch and more urgent tone. The role of the left hand is strong in this work, underpinning the melodies with a powerful dance rhythm that weakens only in the coda.

A playful second theme comes in, trailed by another very dissonant sliding figure in a sharp rhythm. These are repeated, leading to the return of the opening tune, which is then varied by an elaborate accompaniment in an agitated tone. A surprising episode interrupts the kaleidoscopic texture, consisting of a weird, wailing unison passage followed by a phrase in a more solemn rhythm, pulling this soaring work firmly back to earth for a deeply meaningful moment. A new and passionate melodic phrase in two parts, marked by Chopin to be played *con anima,* comes in, with the first phrase in major and the second in minor. Chopin moves these freely through several keys before the playfully sliding second portion of the second theme returns at last to the interwoven melodies of the opening, from which we feel we have traveled a great distance.

The beautiful, more elaborately varied incarnation is heard, leading to the long coda, built of a chain of phrases that rise a little, then fall more. The left hand contains a hypnotically repeated bass note, known as a pedal point, over which the harmony gradually sinks. The melody pauses as if for breath while the rhythm of the left begins to slow, as this magical work fades out on a mournful phrase condensed from the coda's falling melody that seems to hang in the air.

Composed in 1837, the four dances that comprise op. 30 are carefully arranged in ascending intensity. From the quiet work that opens the set to the driving energy of the second, then to the big, outgoing no. 3, everything leads up to the fourth, a stupendous piece that puts Chopin's immense powers on full display.

Though rarely heard, the C minor Mazurka is a fine work of a meditative cast with a lyrical middle section. It ends on a somber reiteration of its main phrase. The B minor Mazurka that follows has a more dancelike feeling, but also one of the boldest harmonic profiles in the entire series. It opens with an innocent tune in B minor, but the second subject pushes ahead with urgency over an accompaniment that shifts harmony with astonishing speed and flexibility. This brings the piece to a simpler, temporizing third theme in A major, where it rests before plunging ahead with the harmonically unstable second theme to an ending in a defiant F-sharp minor, hardly normal for a work nominally in B minor. This is an excellent example of a mazurka that travels musical and emotional distances of which the straightforward opening gives no hint.

Were it not for the C-sharp minor Mazurka that ends the set, the third, in D-flat major, might have served very well as its climax. This long, complex, soulful piece in four sections begins with an impressive introduction that suggests the cry of a caller setting the rhythm for the dancers. The first theme, reminiscent of the lush first tune of the E major Mazurka, op. 6, no. 3, explodes with great splendor, but unlike the earlier melody, this displays a marked tendency to pull immediately into the minor key and lower its volume, enriching the work with an ambiguity absent from its predecessor. The second dance theme, marked *con anima,* is indeed soulful and passionate, and is notable for some rhythmic shifts that are unexpected and refreshing. It is also decorated with some vocally styled flourishes before it leads into the more reserved third theme. As the fourth theme, which is a variant of the second, quiets down, rumbles are heard in the bass that look back to the opening calls; the first theme bursts back onto the scene, ending this generously proportioned dance into which Chopin poured so much rich material.

A drooping phrase in a suggestive rhythm marks the opening of the C-sharp minor Mazurka, the dance of the spirit that concludes the op. 30 set, track 14 on the CD. The first theme comes in immediately (0:09) over a throbbing accompaniment of arpeggiated chords that suggests a guitar. Unusual combinations of adjectives need to coexist to describe this melody, but they must include *melancholy* and *ecstatic,* along with *earthy, ethereal, ghostly, ineffably soulful,* and *utterly sublime.* The tune reaches up (0:19), finding a joy in dance so profound that both it and the accompaniment must pause (0:22). But it starts again, reaching yet higher to notes decorated by exquisite fiorature that again sound like a guitarist picking out a few high notes (0:40, 0:43, and 0:47), after which it pauses from high emotion once more.

The second theme appears (0:58) over a snapping bass that again clearly evokes a guitar, a tune with a sharper rhythmic profile and marked by brooding trills (1:08 and 1:35). Expressing what seemed inexpressible, the third melody (1:52), in a major mode, binds joy and sorrow inseparably, building quickly to a big climax (2:05); the episode from its appearance through the climax (2:34) is repeated. The introductory passage returns (2:53), followed by the first dance (3:01). The coda (3:44), which employs a falling harmonic progression forbidden to composers who follow textbooks (3:44 through 3:56), is one of Chopin's boldest tone paintings: a fantastic fade-out after which the last few notes sound like the guitar player dropping his last few notes. While it may be unwise to suggest scenarios for an abstract musical work, it is not unreasonable to picture a boozy guitarist playing at twilight for an equally potted dancer, and the sound of Chopin's ghostly guitarist makes spectral or visionary interpretations viable as well. Chopin set greater goals for some of the later mazurkas, but he never topped this one.

The first and last of the four op. 33 Mazurkas (1838) carry the unusual tempo indication of *mesto*—sad. While neither work seems sadder than some of the other dances in the series (for example, the A minor, op. 17, no. 4; the E minor, op. 41, no. 2; or the F minor, op. 68, no. 4), Chopin's use of the term may reflect his state of mind. Certainly the first mazurka of the set, in G-sharp minor, is anything but cheerful, sounding far more like a meditation than a dance. The rising second theme is marked *appassionato,* and the work ends gloomily with a quiet statement of the opening theme.

The D major Mazurka, op. 33, no. 2, is on the other hand probably the most high-spirited of all. It opens with a frisky, whirling tune over a left-hand accompaniment strong enough for a waltz. It calms just a bit in the middle section, which also contains a hypnotic passage in a strange rhythm. The coda speeds the tempo dizzyingly, ending the work in a brilliant run high on the keyboard, which Debussy may well have had in his mind when writing the even more dazzling passage that ends *Les collines d'anacapri,* the fifth from his first book of Preludes for the piano. The tiny, tear-stained C major Mazurka that follows presents the curious phenomenon of a major-key work that sounds sad, with an opening section so rhythmically ambiguous that in some perfectly legitimate performances, the beat can be hard to make out. The middle section in A-flat major is more firmly stated.

As in the three previous sets, the op. 33 dances have been leading up to a big piece as the climactic work; this suite climaxes with no. 4 in B minor, one of the longest of all the mazurkas. Conceived by Chopin on an epic scale, it contains so many emotions that the *mesto* marking at its head seems incongruous. The opening melody has a fine tang and is followed by a mysterious passage with a droning quality. There is a then a magnificent, leaping passage, in a different key and almost grandiose in character. The third theme is one of greatest melodies in these dances, so richly emotional that it is almost—but not quite— schmaltzy. The leaping episode returns, trailed by a curious passage for the left hand in which one of the characters in the drama seems to be dancing alone. The opening melody comes back, and there is a brief but highly effective coda, as this huge choreographic poem ends on a splendid rhythmic gesture.

Reversing the usual order, the huge C-sharp minor Mazurka (third of the five in that most important key for mazurkas) opens the op. 41 set, composed over 1838 and '39. This mazurka—like op. 50, no. 3, the next one in C-sharp minor—carries the tempo marking *maestoso* (majestic), unusual for a folk dance but speaking volumes about Chopin's ambitions for these works. This powerful dance opens majestically enough with a bare statement of the rhythm that will pervade it from start to finish. The accompaniment slips in beneath; a grand turning theme rounds out the first group. A more lyrical theme appears, trailed by another rising thematic element in a powerful rhythm. The first theme comes back veiled in ghostly harmony, and the themes are subjected to a kind of symphonic development before leading into two climaxes: the first lyrical but brief, the second and far bigger a gripping apotheosis of the opening phrase. A long, stern coda concludes this mazurka, which more than any of the series resembles the polonaises in its scope and spirit.

The second Mazurka of op. 41 in E minor (track 15) shares with the other two mazurkas on the CD a profoundly poetic nature but has less rhythmic drive and consequently less feeling of the dance. It is instead an agonized testament of Chopin's longing for the homeland he would never see again, unmatched for its intensity in the composer's output.

The work begins with a plain statement of the motto that rules it from start to finish: a sorrowful Wagnerian theme that in eight bars speaks volumes of grief, ending with a chaste phrase (0:19) that suggests dance but takes no steps. The entire opening sequence is then repeated. A change fills the atmosphere at 0:51 as a B sounds deep in the bass, a pedal point that will run through the entire length of the extraordinary middle section. The harmony changes to B major, as a tune that hovers obsessively around a single note (D-sharp, starting at 0:54) appears. Anyone who has experienced loss may recognize in it the agony of recollection: a specific emotion never expressed with greater economy, accuracy, or power. These come from the rigidity with which Chopin grips the B in the left hand (0:51, 0:59, 1:08, 1:16, 1:42, 1:50, 2:00, and 2:08) and the D-sharp in the right (fifty-five times from 0:54 to 2:17) as the lovely, tormented melody coils and uncoils sweetly between them (1:00, 1:18, 1:50, and 2:08).

A new tune appears at 1:26, the most dancelike moment at the very heart of the work, and then the gripping middle section recurs in its entirety (1:42 to 2:17) when Chopin introduces a crescendo (2:14) as the opening motto recurs (2:18), implacable in woe. The first dance theme is heard once more (2:38) as the work ends in desolation beyond comfort. No one would dare call Chopin a miniaturist after hearing this overpowering work, which happens to say everything it needs to in just over three minutes in Idil Biret's leisurely rendition but carries an infinity of longing—*Tristan und Isolde* contains no more than this.

The third and fourth mazurkas of the opus are nearly as wonderful as the first two; Chopin was at the height of his powers in this set, perhaps the greatest one of all. The B major Marzurka that comes next is another dance accompanied by a guitar (like op. 7, no. 3, and op. 30, no. 4), but where those are somber and melancholy, this is wild and giddy. It opens with an unmistakable, aggressive strumming presented as a motto—like in op. 41, no. 2, but of completely different character—and then the racing theme, which performs some of Chopin's most fantastic harmonic acrobatics, leaping madly between keys. The guitar recurs throughout, ending the work softly with its unforgettable motto. Again typical for a mazurka in A-flat major, the final dance of the set begins with an innocent melody so thoroughly modeled as to seem sculpted. Typically, the second theme has more drive, and the work ends perhaps most exquisitely of all the mazurkas on an open-ended reiteration of the second theme that seems to hover motionlessly.

The op. 50 Mazurkas (1842) is the first of the remaining four sets published in Chopin's lifetime, all in groups of three, all large in scale and immensely sophisticated. The G major Mazurka that opens the set begins with a tune so big and openhearted that the listener expects the remainder of the piece to follow suit, but while remaining sweet, its second half turns to A minor. Following another effective left-hand tune reminiscent of the cello (or more likely the double bass) over shifting harmonies in the right, there intrudes a distinctly ominous passage. It passes quickly but returns abruptly again; the double bass comes back for the coda, which contains shifts between G major and G minor, ending this unusual and interesting work in ambiguous depths at which the sunny opening made no hint. The A-flat major Mazurka that follows starts with a mellow introduction before the warm and very memorable first melody enters. A middle episode in the strong, hopping rhythm of the dance provides contrast, and the original tune returns to end the work calmly and without ceremony.

The epic C-sharp minor Mazurka, op. 50, no. 3, is perhaps the most elaborate and ambitious of the series: abstract, poetic, and grand. Chopin pulls out all the technical stops here, using varied material, a subtle developmental structure, his most advanced harmonies, and brilliant counterpoint to create a poignant Polish tone poem. He perhaps surpasses the previous C-sharp minor Mazurka (op. 41, no. 1) with a work that is both more graceful and expressive, and the final C-sharp minor dance from op. 63, which is lovely but smaller in scale.

An arching phrase in the right hand that begs to be choreographed opens the work on a magical note. It is answered contrapuntally by the left; an intense but still graceful dance melody floats up, then down;

and the opening group ends with a widely spaced phrase in a sharper rhythm. The second theme begins with a fiery statement of the mazurka rhythm, after which a soothing rocking theme appears over a broadly flowing accompaniment. This group ends with a tune based on the wide melody that concluded the opening sequence, but in a simpler profile and slightly easier rhythm, leading to a long episode in which this theme is played out over gently shifting harmony.

It begins to pick up momentum, however, winding up again at the note (G-sharp) with which the mazurka began, where it pauses majestically, as though having rediscovered its true character and purpose, before spinning out the glistening opening group once more. But instead of bringing back the simple episode, Chopin combines the themes of the first group in shifting chromatic harmony in a symphonic expansion quite different from the gentle passage it replaces. It builds to a climax that is powerful without overstatement, leading into a contrapuntal coda that mirrors the opening. This work of oceanic grandeur ends on a proud cadence in the mazurka rhythm.

The op. 56 trio of 1845 proceed along much the same lines as the previous set, with a work in B major that opens bravely like the G major Mazurka of op. 50 but also betrays instability—in this case at the very beginning, where the melody is sandwiched inside shifting harmonies that leave the listener uncertain as to the key for much longer than is normal. The melody descends gently, then surges upward dramatically to a proud and noble phrase that rounds out the opening section. The next episode consists of scampering figuration over an accompaniment that emphasizes the strong second beat typical of the mazurka; its return ends in a dizzying chromatic descent. This dance is reminiscent of some of the larger works of the same period—notably the B minor Sonata in its use of contrasting but related keys—and of the *Polonaise-fantaisie* in its large scale and swift procession of changing moods. Typically for the three-mazurka sets, the C major Mazurka in the center is the shortest and simplest. It opens with the unmistakable thrum of a bagpipe, over which skips a tune in sharp rhythm. The middle section includes some droning scales that lend an exotic sound.

The C minor Mazurka, op. 56, no. 3, is the longest of all the mazurkas and probably the most difficult to grasp, but one that without question holds a place in the pantheon. Chopin put the work together with immense skill, and it is a great example of his harmonic daring and structural inventiveness, as he moves without strain between keys while building on the most generous scale. The first theme consists of a ruminative melody, not at all danceable, rounded out by a modal phrase. The second theme moves into A-flat major, then swiftly into the distant B major, then to B-flat for the long and powerful middle section that seems more like a procession than a dance. The opening theme returns and is developed briefly in the rhythmic shape taken from the central episode, leading into the long coda, at the beginning of which the dance impulse briefly emerges before winding down to a brooding conclusion in C major. The C minor Mazurka contains no big outbursts or climaxes to draw the listener in; one must go to it, confident that patient listening will be rewarded.

Composed in 1845, the Mazurkas of op. 59 are essays in Chopin's last style: lush, fluent, illuminated by inner fire. A beautiful dance in A minor that begins simply but moves on to reveal unexpected depths opens the set. First, a sinuous melody passes from right hand to left and back, heavily decorated with grace notes and trills. The central episode in A major has a more solid rhythmic profile, but its melting melody sounds like a free continuation of the opening. The work's two climaxes are small and delicate; in the coda, the theme is transferred broodingly to the left hand, and it ends on a simple but exquisite upward gesture. This is a haunting work that once insinuated into the mind can be hard to dislodge.

The elegant A-flat major work that follows opens with one of those ripe melodies that the key always suggested to Chopin. The dance moves with ease through various keys and chromatic detours before ending on brief but breathtaking passagework and four simple chords. The great F-sharp minor Mazurka that represents the climax of the set opens with a spirited, swirling melody that clearly shows its descent from the very first Mazurka, op. 6, no. 1, in the same key, but somehow purged of all flesh. The middle episode displays an ineffable sweetness, and the section ends on a fantastic passage in plangent harmony and jogging rhythm that is one of Chopin's most unforgettable inspirations. The opening melody rises gently from the bass, followed by the entire first thematic group. Knowing a good thing when he wrote it, Chopin introduces the jogging tune into the coda. Like most of the mazurkas, this one ends without the least rhetoric.

The op. 63 set, composed in 1846, contains the last three mazurkas published in Chopin's lifetime. The scale of the pieces is now somewhat smaller, and the tone is more melancholy, befitting the composer's deteriorating health, but the works show no diminution of his powers. The first of the dances, in B major, opens with a radiant theme, last in the joyous line of the E major, op. 6, no. 3; the B-flat major mazurkas op. 7, no. 1, and op. 17, no. 2; the D-flat major, op. 30, no. 3; and the G major, op. 50, no. 1. This moves into a more flowing line over a trotting rhythm, followed by a brave leap to A major and a simple but exquisite second theme in which Chopin jumps from one register to another, ending in a mock rustic phrase that is actually very sophisticated. A sad melody that falls, rises, and then falls gracefully once more opens the F minor Mazurka that is the centerpiece of the set, but the second theme glows with an inextinguishable inner fire, making the little work very moving indeed. And the last of the great C-sharp minor Mazurkas, the last also of this set, is graceful rather than heroic, in character not unlike the op. 64 Waltz in the same key written the following year. It ends with a display of contrapuntal writing in which Chopin shows off his easy mastery, a treatment that also happens to suit the melody very well.

As noted, the final two sets of mazurkas published as opp. 67 and 68 came out six years after Chopin's death. Some of the works were known to Chopin's pupils, to whom he had taught them; they were assembled and published by his friend Julian Fontana. As a result, they are random assortments of old and new dances—some charming, others melancholy, none at quite the highest level—ordered without the art Chopin applied to the sets he himself sent for publication.

Op. 67 begins with a happy work in G major from 1835 that opens with a forceful droning figure imitating a bagpipe. The main melodic group consists of a fine tune, followed by a figure that skips up and down the keyboard. The bagpipe is heard again in the central section, and the end is spirited. The G minor work that follows is dated by experts to 1848 or '49, which would make it one of Chopin's last compositions, if not the very last. It is predictably sad but still melodious, and not of great complexity; but the middle section is memorable, ending with a strange passage for right hand alone that leads back to the main melody.

The C major dance that comes third is a work from 1835. Despite the key, the opening tune is sweetly melancholy. It is repeated in harmony, as though sung first by one person and then two people who know it well and have sung it together many times; the middle section continues this pattern. Chopin composed the A minor Mazurka that concludes the set in 1846. As the late date suggests, it is a sophisticated work, full of chromatic harmony; the middle section extends the opening tune in a fervent A major. This is probably the finest of the group, and it is unclear why Chopin chose not to publish it. Perhaps he couldn't find a place that satisfied him in any of the earlier sets.

The op. 68 set opens with three fine early works and ends with a late dance of the most tragic character. First comes a lusty C major Mazurka dated to c. 1830. It opens with a fantastic stamping figure over a droning bass, followed by a leaping theme, then a sweet tune at its center. The A minor Mazurka that follows (c. 1827) is the earliest work in these two posthumous sets. It opens with a dreamy, hypnotic melody that displays the young Chopin's early mastery. The middle section in A major sounds like the call and response at a square dance, reminding the listener of the mazurka's rustic origins.

The F major Mazurka that comes next is yet another small-scale treasure from c. 1830, which opens with a heartfelt melody, leading eventually to a charming middle section in which Chopin delicately renders a droning bass, over which a scurries a fleeting but brilliant impression of a shepherd's pipe. This marvelous episode is over in about twelve seconds, in yet another demonstration of the composer's rare skill at making his point without beating listeners over the head.

There is no mistaking the sorrow of the F minor Mazurka that concludes this quartet: from the drooping opening melody above a light accompaniment to the chromatic shifts of the delicate passagework to the open ending, there is no joy in this gem dated to c. 1846.

Two more mazurkas without opus numbers of their own are part of the standard canon. Both are in A minor. One, dedicated to Chopin's friend and pupil Emile Gaillard, is a surging, articulate work from 1840, with a middle section in biting octaves and an imaginative coda that ends the work in a long trill. The other, nicknamed "Notre Temps" (Our Times) for the 1842 anthology to which Chopin contributed it, is dated to c. 1839. It is a thoughtful and eloquent composition in which the left hand carries the melody and the harmony rides above in the right. The middle section in A major continues in the pensive vein of the opening episode, which returns to conclude the piece.

A survey of the mazurkas reveals their infinite variety and ability to surprise: one continually discovers new beauties in all of them and is constantly settling on a new favorite. Consider, for example, how many begin plainly, simply, or innocently and then proceed to cover vast harmonic and emotional ground; or think of the marvelous, unrhetorical eloquence with which all of them end. The most rustic-sounding moments are achieved by subtle sophistication. Throughout the series, Chopin creates his effects at the highest and most refined level. The eternal freshness of the mazurkas derives from the Polish flavor of the melodies and harmonies, setting them apart from the rest of Chopin's work where the Italian melodic influence dominates.

Among the fifty-one, these nine are perhaps the greatest, at least in scope: F minor, op. 7, no. 3; A minor, op. 17, no. 4; B-flat minor, op. 24, no. 4; C-sharp minor, op. 30, no. 4 (track 14); B minor, op. 33, no. 4; C-sharp minor, op. 41, no. 1; C-sharp minor, op. 50, no. 3; C minor, op. 56, no. 3; and F-sharp minor, op. 63, no. 3. But as the two of the three on the CD that are not on this list readily show, there is so much that is wonderful in dances other than the big nine that it would be a terrible mistake to focus only on the supposed "greatest." The world would be far poorer without the soul and spirit shown in works like op. 6, nos. 1 and 2, or the fleeting, wild vision that is last in the op. 6 set—and so on, through the rest of the series. The best way to get to know these extraordinary soul-dances is to listen to them all. Here and there parts will reach out, and before long you will have your own favorites: there are worlds contained in every one.

The Ballades

A s a group, the four ballades are Chopin's greatest compositions in a large form. Their preeminence within a body of work as consistently strong as Chopin's is widely accepted and of long standing; their stature has rarely been challenged, although the greatness of the fourth, op. 52, came to be recognized only gradually. It is now with considerable justification widely regarded as Chopin's supreme masterwork, a peerless distinction indeed.

The ballades arrest the listener's attention with their obvious power and beauty, but they are highly complex musical organisms as well, with daring narrative structures and openly dramatic temperaments. All are built of two contrasting themes, which Chopin plays off against each other. This suggests a kinship between the various forms of the ballades (no two are precisely alike) and the sonata, but in fact, the standard sonata movement and Chopin's ballade part ways after being founded on two themes. Chopin's ballades are equally lyric and dramatic, pitched toward a climactic ending, which in three of the four ballades is manifestly tragic; moreover, the composer devised a different structure for each, based on the thematic material and his goals for each work as a whole.

Of all Chopin's works, the ballades are probably the largest in conception, their potent dramatic impulses driving them from first note to last. These dramatic qualities roughly equal those of the scherzos, but the forms differ, with the ballades being somewhat freer. Chopin's melodic imagination in the ballades is magnificent as always, but it would be incorrect as well as unfair to describe their melodies as superior to those in his other works. Some of the thematic material,

especially in op. 52, is strikingly reserved, at least in the early iterations. It is through their structural use—the ways Chopin applies them
in narrative, lyrical, and dramatic guises—that they reach their peaks
of eloquence. All the ballades are very difficult to play, requiring a high
level of pianistic technique, and are perennial favorites with artists and
audiences.

The form and title seem to be of Chopin's own invention. There
appear to be no instrumental works with the title before his. Perhaps
only those by Brahms afterward are superb and well worth knowing,
but they are not modeled on Chopin's, and they have a more rigid form.
Nor, frankly, do they possess the same power and sweep. Liszt composed works with the same title, as did Grieg and Fauré, all influenced
by Chopin. But as with the mazurka, the ballade is Chopin's own form,
and in it he reigns supreme.

None tells a specific tale, but all four bear out the title's hint that a
story is being related. As the title suggests, the inspiration for the ballade is the *ballad,* a narrative in which a story is told in verse, often set
off by a repeated refrain. In the earliest versions, the songs were danced
to—*ballare* meaning to dance in Italian. In French operas of the day,
ballades are narrative arias. The Italian word for the form is *ballata;
Quest o quella,* the Duke of Mantua's very first aria in Verdi's *Rigoletto*
is perhaps the most familiar example. It is also written in a skipping
rhythm similar to the one Chopin employs in his ballades. The musical
equivalent of the iambic foot in poetry, this pattern is the short-long
(or unstressed-stressed) rhythm that most resembles speech.

The ballad form can be found in many settings of lyrics by German
and Austrian composers from the late eighteenth and early nineteenth
centuries (Schubert's *Erlkönig* is the best known example). Other bal-
lads affect a deliberately stiff, archaic tone that looks back to the Middle
Ages—a popular artistic subject in the early nineteenth century as
evidenced by the novels of Sir Walter Scott as well as countless opera
plots set during the period, including Wagner's *Lohengrin* and Verdi's
Il trovatore. The first of Brahms's ballades is modeled on a specific poem,
the gruesome and repetitious *Edward,* which starts and ends with a
refrain echoed quite clearly by the music.

Chopin was thought to have found the inspiration for the ballades in poems by his countryman Adam Mickiewicz, but there are no epigraphs or extramusical suggestions in the scores to back up that claim. Chopin's brilliant innovation was to break away from a specific story while retaining the narrative posture, thereby allowing his own imagination—as well as those of his listeners—free rein. As a result, his ballades display a breadth, universality, and with the exception of the third, a tragic power denied to Brahms and even to Schubert, tied as they were to texts. Chopin's ballades are best regarded as music, abstract and pure.

Published in 1836, the Ballade no. 1 in G minor, op. 23, was once thought, like the Scherzo no. 1, to have been written in 1831 or '32. Now both works, enormously powerful and large in scale, are assigned to 1834 and '35. The G minor Ballade cost the young composer considerable struggle, the result of which is a masterpiece of imperishable but fully justified popularity with musicians and audiences. It is a work of impassioned lyricism and high drama, as well as a great virtuoso showpiece. In it, the lines along which the next three ballades will run are broadly laid out.

A powerful introduction in a slow tempo opens the work on a Homeric note, suggesting a poet striking the lyre to summon his listeners' attention before recounting an old and tragic tale. The passage ends on a long, unusually dissonant chord, before the opening theme—dancelike, inward, and melancholy—is introduced. As Chopin subjects the arching opening melody to eloquent expansion, the tune moves into the left hand, before the opening group finally ends in dreamy but passionate fioratura. An urgent, compressed version of the opening melody marked *agitato* presses the drama ahead into a long passage built of figuration that swirls and boils, eventually calming down over gentle chords reminiscent of horn calls as the music settles magically into E-flat major for the second theme: a glistening, vocally styled melody presented over a bejeweled accompaniment.

Its second portion contains a swirling figure that is actually another version of the opening theme, which soon reappears in its original guise as a crescendo moving into the triumphant but never bombastic statement of the second theme in all its magnificence, now in A major. An energetic passage leads to an episode in which the second part of the first theme is restated, essentially as a waltz. More difficult passage-work precedes a reiteration of the glorious second theme in a deeper register of its home key of E-flat major, over a boiling Alberti bass. The curling melodic figure that concluded the second thematic group reappears, revealing its close kinship to the opening melody and leading into vaporous passagework where both melody and texture thin out ominously. The opening melody returns as a refrain, now in a threatening tone, as Chopin builds tension by gripping the same harmony and entering on a long crescendo, a strategy he would use again in the lead-up to the coda of the C-sharp minor Scherzo, op. 39.

A colossal passage marked *appassionato* hurls the work into the ferocious coda, which is made of entirely new material. This displays a whiplash fury with a distinctly Slavic rhythmic snap before the last page. Here, long, raging scales are interspersed with somber pauses, quiet chords, and an intense recitative-like figure (anticipating those that also end the Nocturne in B major, op. 32, no. 1) that represents the final incarnation of the curling open melody. A torrent of octaves and thunderous chords bring the G minor Ballade to a fierce and tragic end.

The Ballade no. 2, op. 38, possesses, in addition to the normal helpings of power and beauty, a fascinating structure of exceptional originality. The work is in two keys, beginning in F major and ending in A minor, but it is not comparable to the Scherzo no. 2, op. 31, in B-flat minor/D-flat major, or the Fantasy op. 49, which uses F minor and A-flat major as its single tonal home base. The two key signatures of the second Ballade—the F major in which it begins, identified throughout with the innocent opening tune, and A minor, with its stormy second theme as well as a terrifying third melodic sequence that opens the coda—are always in conflict, never interchangeable.

The first three-and-a-half pages of the score bear some formal resemblance to the Scherzo no. 3, op. 39 (track 12), Chopin's other big work of 1839 in which the two main themes seem to inhabit separate worlds. The scherzo strictly carries that scheme through to the end, keeping the ideas apart, until the coda, based on new material, takes over. Of course, once both themes have been set forth, it is impossible to hear one without thinking of the other, but Chopin never places them into direct contact. The op. 38 Ballade begins with its two ideas presented in the starkest possible contrast, but as soon as both have been presented, they contaminate each other, and the remainder of the work is a playing out of the struggle between them. In the coda of the second Ballade, a crucial new idea is presented, but Chopin brings back both of the original themes (the second followed by the first) to end the work.

It begins, however, with one of Chopin's gentlest tunes: a folk-like melody in a rocking, pastoral rhythm. Cast in exceptionally long phrases, there is considerable harmonic shifting beneath the nearly motionless surface. Rhythmically, the opening has many important relatives in Chopin's output, from the second themes of the Nocturne in G major, op. 37, no. 2, and the Barcarolle, op. 60, to the crucial second theme of the Ballade no. 4 (track 16), all of which share to varying degrees its steady pulse and slippery harmonic underpinning. The tune comes to a point of stasis, after which a soft arpeggio gently signals its end. There is the briefest of pauses before the second theme—in A minor and at the new tempo *presto con fuoco* (very fast and fiery)—crashes in. Consisting of hammering octaves in the left hand under slashing passagework in the right, its entrance is terrifying, like that of a dangerous character in a drama, offering the greatest possible contrast to the gentle, long-spun opening melody. Its effect is much like that of the raging middle section of the F major Nocturne, op. 15, no. 1, which also invades a tranquil opening, but this is yet more violent.

The second part of the thematic group consists of powerful, richly harmonized chords in the rhythm of the opening theme over a running accompaniment, finally settling down in a magnificent passage in which steady chords in the right hand attempt to quell the turbulence in the left. This, however, continues to threaten in a sequence of long, grumbling runs. The gentle opening theme returns, its innocence now lost, interrupted by expressive pauses, plaintive minor-key inflections, and finally a more angry quality as it is dominated by big, anxious chords in a rising sequence. Things settle down briefly once more, as the rising chords lead to a return of the second theme, here in D minor. The fast-moving right hand flows above a troubled version of the gentle opening melody, now thundered in octaves in the bass, as innocence and violence are tragically united. Four burning trills lead to the astonishing closing passage in A minor, marked *agitato* and very agitated indeed, in which a panicked right hand expresses terror and rage with chattering short notes in close harmony.

The second theme storms back in with even greater fury than before, ending on the jagged snap of an arpeggiated chord. The opening phrase is heard in pathetic A minor one last time, and three quiet chords end this bold work in deep sorrow. Op. 38 is dedicated to "Monsieur Robert Schumann," returning Schumann's compliment of inscribing to Chopin his *Kreisleriana,* op. 16 (1838), a great early masterwork for the piano. Chopin's dedication was nothing more than a polite gesture. He had little personal regard for Schumann—whose admiration for Chopin's music was immense and whose early critical praise helped pave Chopin's way into the pantheon—and despised his music.

The Ballade no. 3 in A-flat major, op. 47 (1841), was once the best loved of the four. Since around the middle of the twentieth century, it has yielded pride of place to the fourth Ballade; but its popularity has never really diminished, thanks to its strength of character and radiant beauties, which familiarity cannot dim. It stands in relation to the other ballades as the E major Scherzo does to its companions: where the others are dramatic and usually tragic, it is joyful; where Ballades nos. 1, 2, and 4 end in disaster, it concludes in unmistakable triumph. Not that it lacks drama: the climax of the second theme is pretty aggressive, but it is trumped by the apotheosis of the aristocratic and highly memorable first theme, one of Chopin's great A-flat major melodies, that opens the work in a lovely, long span, passing elegantly between the hands.

Sharply accented octaves form its second part, and a graceful, trill-laden figure that reaches high and low on the keyboard rounds it out. The second group begins with an accompaniment in the right hand, a simple enough figure that projects a slight limp—a hint of deliberate awkwardness—as the second theme appears, sounding gracious and even mellifluous. But before long it builds into a more earnest passage, where the theme is stated forcefully in F minor above the limping accompaniment, now thundered in the bass. While this dies down, the tone of the transitional episode that follows remains serious. As a result, the listener hears the second theme with more respect when it returns.

An entirely new melody follows that reprise: a soaring waltz, high-spirited, ecstatic, and graceful. This opens out into a brief, impassioned variant of the second theme above a swelling Alberti bass. The second theme is heard one last time in its original incarnation before the key changes to C-sharp minor. The accompaniment picks up in intensity as the second theme drives to a fierce climax, garbed in whiplash pianistic figuration. The rapid accompaniment surges along, palpably seeking release, as fragments of both the opening theme and the second melody break above it like surf on a powerful tide.

Finally the big climax—one of Chopin's most magnificent—approaches clearly, as the opening theme blazes in all its glory. But as Charles Rosen has pointed out, Chopin reins it in by means of shortening and dramatic key changes to create an excitement and ecstasy that neither an expansion, which would surely contain at least a hint of pomposity, nor a repetition could ever match. A series of fat chords leads into the short but spectacular coda, built on the high-flying waltz. This great work, while intellectually complex and challenging, is also eminently satisfying to the listener's emotions. It is another of Chopin's deservedly popular masterpieces.

Chopin wrote the F minor Ballade, op. 52 (track 16 on the CD), over 1842 and '43; it was published in the latter year. This complex and difficult work was at first poorly understood and even regarded as inferior to the first three. But by the middle of the twentieth century, it was being performed regularly by Vladimir Horowitz and Arthur Rubinstein, two great if very different Chopin players, and recorded by them and others. This allowed musicians and musical scholars to hear the work and reassess it. Its stock rose quickly to sovereign status, not just within Chopin's output, but as one of the towering achievements of nineteenth-century European music. Some latter-day contrarians claim to favor the F minor Fantasy, op. 49; the Poloniase-fantaisie, op. 61 has become fashionable as well. But neither work, great and beautiful as each may be, has the overwhelming cumulative effect of the F minor Ballade, which grows out of its brilliant and original structure.

Indeed, it is Chopin's form, which is rigorous but full of surprises, that makes the F minor Ballade fly. The most helpful way of looking at this structure is to think of it as two themes with variations, opened by an introduction, concluded by a coda of different material, and interspersed with three brief episodes. The introduction that begins the ballade is delicate: all hesitation, half-tints, and sighs. But it is rich in harmony, hinting at what will come. The first theme enters at 0:36, austerely narrow in range but deeply expressive over a graceful, waltzlike accompaniment. Its second portion is notable for two alternating notes followed by three repeated ones (0:47). The opening theme—very memorable, and which Chopin will soon make certain the listener remembers anyway—is repeated at 0:57. Its first variation begins at 1:38, with the opening phrase of the theme enlarged only slightly by decoration at 1:44, 2:02, and 2:26. It is normal for first-time listeners to wonder what to make of these minute expansions, so little do they seem to add, but Chopin is branding the tune into the listener's consciousness and preparing the way for more passionate and elaborately decorated variants, soon to come.

Just as the music threatens monotony in the form of a second variation, however, Chopin introduces at 2:39 the first episode, a spectral passage in a steady processional rhythm that floats away from any key (the left-hand portion played alone is a stunning anticipation of Debussy's piano sound), amplifying the strange, dreamlike quality of the music. This moment passes as the third variation of the first theme begins (3:11). Here Chopin starts with the second half, however, expanding the narrow alternating and repeated notes with a reach for higher notes (3:16), trills (3:26), and the entrance of a second voice at 3:30. As the range of the theme widens, its eloquence also begins to grow. But Chopin thins the texture severely once more, and at 3:47 there is a hesitation just before this variation ends.

The glamorous fourth variation, beginning at 3:55, makes explicit all the textural richness and passion at which the prior one only hinted. Both left and right hand now perform virtuoso feats, as the first theme is draped in sumptuous harmonies (note the gorgeous chord at 4:14, repeated at 4:17), enhanced also by an intense hammering figure (4:09) that will recur several times later with even more vehemence. The left hand begins to thunder at 4:11, while the right plays the theme with nearly swooning passion. This builds toward a climax (4:25 to 4:40), which is interrupted by the second episode, a fleeting passage in which the first theme is broken into glittering figuration before disappearing entirely. But we are now aware of the deep emotion lurking behind the surface of the quiet first theme.

The second theme—one of Chopin's great rocking tunes, marked by an insidious harmonic sideslipping that subtly undermines its apparent stolidity—appears at 4:55. Like the first theme, it is extremely contained here in its initial appearance; unlike its companion, it will be treated to only one variation, but that of immense potency. This, improbably, is the climactic tune of the ballade. Except for its length, the continued theme would be easy to mistake for another one of the passing episodes. Note, however, its calm, deliberate character with many long-held chords and pauses (5:05, 5:13, 5:35, and 5:44), its most active moment a quietly turning figure at 5:24.

The high point of the melody comes at 5:13 and is repeated at 5:35, but even these presentations are so restrained that it is only later, after one has heard its climactic incarnation, that its prominence in the profile of the melody becomes clear. It is also worthwhile to compare the waltzlike rhythm and sculpted melody of the melancholy first theme with the solidity of this one. The second theme is followed by the beautiful third episode: a fleet, dancelike passage (5:54) that sounds like leaves tumbling before the wind and includes the hammering figure at 6:02.

After this comes a transition starting at 6:39 that can perhaps be viewed as another episode and is quite possibly the most astonishing music Chopin wrote. This much-admired passage refers to the opening theme, but here floated above a choreographically graceful left-hand accompaniment containing what sounds like horn calls (6:19 through 6:24). The tone darkens noticeably from 6:37, where the opening theme asserts itself more insistently, rising like a vision through a misty accompaniment we can now recognize as the introduction, into which the theme is densely woven (6:44). But instead of the first theme taking over, we realize that the introduction itself is the vision. (7:00) when it is heard complete, as delicate as before but bereft of its innocence and now saturated in minor-key inflections (7:13). There is a rest, followed by a ghostly cadenza (7:28) where we pause one last time for breath.

Chopin himself seems to hesitate before embarking on the fifth variation of the first theme (7:38), which is written in the contrapuntal form called a canon, assuming its original form for the last time at 8:15. The sixth and final variation appears at 8:40, with the theme lavishly decorated but set forth in broken, desperately declaimed phrases over a broadly sweeping Alberti bass, a passage reminiscent of the nocturnes or even the slow movements of the concertos, but in this context surpassingly passionate and beautiful—an operatic apotheosis of the first theme. There is a short, surging transition, beginning at 9:09. At 9:17, above rolling scales of tidal force, the second theme appears in full majesty, so stunning that loudness would only detract from its intensity. The passions that have been held in check for so long can no longer be restrained: this is the point at which madness breaches the work's carefully maintained structure. Both hands break into mighty arpeggios, and the keyboard seems to liquefy from passion (9:34) in one of the most stupendous moments in the piano literature. Now the second theme crashes in more violently (9:38), as the theme and accompaniment surge ahead in wildest emotion, prescient of Wagner at his best (9:47 though 10:10).

Finally, Chopin's elaborate form collapses under the onslaught of the passion, rage, and terror he has unleashed, as four gigantic arpeggios, strongly reminiscent of those that make up the C minor Etude, op. 25, no. 12, roar across the keyboard (10:12 through 10:19). Then follows another arpeggio, six titanic chords (10:21), yet another furious arpeggio, and eighteen shattering chords with an equally violent reply (10:30), which blast away all traces of what went before. There is a brief pause, followed by six soft and spectral chords (10:36), as a long silence prepares us for the long and brutal coda, made up of new material. In this very difficult passage, listeners might think they can pick out broken fragments of the themes, but these are illusory, being nothing more than basic intervals that could come from anywhere. There is at 11:03 and 11:24 some close, hard writing for the right hand, and a groaning melodic fragment at last rises painfully above the raging of the left hand (11:27 and 11:33). After this the music takes on more shape (11:36) as it sweeps irresistibly to the end; stern chords hold the stage below fierce descending scales (11:44), and the music pours into a terrible boiling low down in the keyboard (11:53). The work ends in four granitic chords.

Chopin's artful management of his thematic material early in the work is what makes its release at the end so devastating. The first-time listener cannot foresee in the inexpressive initial statements of the two main themes the eloquence, high passion, and measureless power of the climaxes; even the episodes seem to have more energy. Not only does the work begin shyly, but that quality pervades it for nearly a third of its twelve-minute length (in Biret's performance, that is; many pianists, although not all, take it a bit faster). Chopin's tight structure seems to guide the two main themes into acting their parts like characters in a play, but it is full of astonishing surprises too. The organic flow as well as the passion and sweep of the music ultimately win us over, as we track the course of the themes from their introverted beginning through utterances that only gradually grow more articulate, until passion overwhelms both—and us with them.

So palpable is the dramatic feeling and flow of the F minor Ballade that it is impossible to listen to the work without wondering what it's about. That two great characters or forces have come into a conflict in which both are finally destroyed is clear, but because it is pure music, the mystery remains intact. If one definition of a great creative artist is the possession of the tragic vision of life and the ability to express that vision, then the mighty drama that is the F minor Ballade is proof, unequivocally and unarguably, of Chopin's tragic vision and of his transcendent greatness as a creator.

The Importance
of Chopin

Chopin's popularity seems indestructible. Neither artists nor their audiences seem to tire of it. In recital, most pianists need to show off their interpretive and technical skills with a Chopin selection; his music seems to be recorded every bit as frequently as it was half a century ago. As you have heard, this is easily explained: most of his music is richly beautiful, memorable, and admirably concise without being at all cramped. Chopin knew as well as any composer and more than most to stop when he'd had his say. As a result, his works are never overlong or tiresome; there's a sense of satisfaction in listening to Chopin. A big, memorable melody will always sell a musical composition. As a melodist, Chopin ranks with the greatest. No tune could be more wildly ecstatic than that of the A-flat Etude, op. 25, no. 1, which opens the selection on the CD, or more passionate but poised than the rich and stately flow of the D-flat major Nocturne, op. 27, no. 2 (track 8). Chopin's joyous moments stand on a level with those of the greatest composers: consider the exuberance of the D major Mazurka, op. 33, no. 2, or the Olympian serenity, reminiscent of Bach, of the Etude in C major, op. 10, no. 7. Or listen to the orgasmic triumph of the Ballade no. 3, op. 47. Aside from the loveliness and familiarity to listeners of much of what he wrote, Chopin speaks in a distinctive voice that is instantly recognizable. With one masterpiece after another forming his oeuvre, Chopin's batting average is perhaps the highest of any great composer's.

Chopin's compositions reveal an unprecedented originality. Emerging from Warsaw with his style fully formed, the young Chopin had few musical ancestors of significance. He absorbed Bach and Mozart completely but sounds only like Chopin. As a model for certain of his own highly memorable tunes, he used the melodies of his contemporary and friend, the opera composer Bellini (whose opera *Norma* contains the famous aria "Casta diva"—"Chaste Goddess"—a vocal nocturne with orchestral and choral accompaniment), but he recast Bellini's long-breathed vocal melodies into idiomatic piano writing. Many of Chopin's greatest compositions—particularly the ballades, scherzos, polonaises, mazurkas, and impromptus—are in highly inventive and effective forms of his own design. While Chopin's style clearly ripened over the course of his career, his early works are mature and completely satisfying to listen to. Chopin found his path early and followed it with the confidence of genius.

But in another sense, Chopin's popularity is baffling, for just beneath the glittering surfaces lurk crosscurrents of dark emotion expressed with a compositional technique that is challenging and tough minded: for every work that sounds positive or cheerful, there are half a dozen that are yearning, sorrowful, brooding, furious, or downright bizarre. The two most famous of Chopin's polonaises are nicknamed "Military" and "Heroic." Both are in bright major keys, and both carry themselves with a splendid swagger; but both stand in the shadows of the gigantic, barbaric, nerve-wracking Polonaise in F-sharp minor (track 10) and the *Polonaise-fantaisie*, the profound and moody masterpiece from late in Chopin's career. What may well be the single best known snatch of classical music in the world is the opening of the third movement of Chopin's Piano Sonata no. 2, the Funeral March that everyone knows at an early age. Although Chopin resented all attempts to apply nonmusical meanings to his work, that sonata—one of his boldest, strangest, and greatest compositions—seems a vast meditation on death. As beautiful as it is, Chopin's music is far from easy.

Chopin died a famous man with his place in the pantheon secure, but that has not prevented some artists and critics, mostly in the decades just before and after the turn of the twentieth century, from undervaluing him. Chopin's pithiness and highly polished surfaces caused some to treat him as a precious musical miniaturist—a laughably parochial approach, long since discredited, that equated Wagnerian length with quality or found it necessary to compare everyone with Beethoven and, of course, to find them lacking. (During the mid-nineteenth century, Mozart suffered from a similar misjudgment for many of the same reasons.)

Chopin is, with Haydn, Mozart, Beethoven, and Wagner, a member of the eternal avant-garde: a daring protomodernist and a direct inspiration for some of the most important composers of the twentieth century, including Bartók, Webern, and above all, Debussy. Chopin's positive influence on these and others is surely as great as that of Wagner, whose giant masterpieces dazzled but also made it obvious that the late romantic style had been pushed to its limit. Unlike Wagner, Chopin was a master of musical compression, expert at cutting fat and condensing many of his works down into musical aphorisms. For composers who followed, his diamond-hard forms were useful guides to the musical future. Alone among the great composers, Chopin restricted his output to the piano. But this limitation has never posed a problem for musicians and listeners, who have always correctly understood it to be a primary source of strength. Chopin took the instrument to its expressive peak, occasionally equaled but never surpassed.

In a way, Chopin's themes are like characters in a drama, who take the stage, say their lines, and then exit. Rhetoric was not Chopin's style: with the notable exceptions of the nocturnes and the Barcarolle, his works rarely begin with long flourishes, nor does he employ lengthy postludes. With a flood of musical ideas at his disposal and a refined sense of proportion, Chopin had no need to drag out thematic material or flog it in triumphant repetition. Some of the preludes and many of the mazurkas seem to start in the middle and end abruptly, or fade in and out cinematically. For Chopin, a piece of short duration was as much an opportunity to say something grand as a larger form. The longest of the notoriously difficult etudes takes five minutes to play—and most are considerably shorter—yet they are heroic in voice and scale.

Chopin has been, is, and will remain popular because of the well-nigh perfect fusion in his music of the lyrical with the dramatic. That penetrating lyricism—combined with one of the most acute dramatic sensibilities in music outside of opera, interpreted through his dense, complex compositional technique—results in music that is sensuously pleasing, intellectually challenging, and powerfully provocative of our emotions. Chopin's importance—his greatness—is built on the firmest musical and artistic ground. Chopin speaks clearly to us because we hear in his textural density the complexity of existence; in his drama, our struggles and tragedies; and in his lyricism, our very own joys and passions.

Notes

Chapter 1. Chopin's Brief Life and Long Death

3   "The composer of": Quoted in Siepmann, *Chopin*, 11.

5   "Leave him": Quoted in Samson, *Cambridge Companion to Chopin*, 167.

5   "with Messers Zywny": Ibid., 166–167.

8   "The most vociferous": Quoted in Siepmann, *Chopin*, 87.

8   "Here is a young": Ibid.

9   "You think I": Quoted in Eisler, *Chopin's Funeral* 48; Orga, *Illustrated Lives*, 72; Schonberg, *Great Pianists*, 144.

9   "Chopin was a": Quoted in Eigeldinger, *Chopin*, 11.

9   "have the body": Ibid., 29.

10   "Chopin's main concern": Ibid., 29.

10   "To encourage me": Ibid., 12.

10   "But this did": Ibid., 167.

11   "Intonation being the": Ibid., 192.

11   "His wonderful playing": Ibid., 272.

12   "the same evening": Ibid., 273.

12   "I could only": Ibid.

12–13   "Liszt is playing": Quoted in Schonberg, *Great Pianists*, 151.

15   "Chopin came to": Quoted in Eigeldinger, *Chopin*, 168–169.

15   "All right": Ibid.

16–17   "His music was": Quoted in Siepmann, *Chopin*, 152.

17   "Art is not": Ibid., 160.

19   "He comes down": Quoted in Szulc, *Chopin in Paris*, 269.

19   "Chopin has broken": Quoted in Siepmann, *Chopin*, 167.

19   "Nothing equals the": Ibid.

20   "Frik-Frik": Quoted in Eisler, *Chopin's Funeral*, 74; Siepmann, *Chopin*, 165, 177.

20   "excessively polite": Quoted in Siepmann, *Chopin*, 178.

21   "This misfortune must": Ibid., 198.

21   "maintain my right": Ibid., 199.

23   "several pianists": Szulc, *Chopin in Paris*, 376.

23   "Panting until dinner": Quoted in Eisler, *Chopin's Funeral*, 187.

23   "gasping and dreaming": Ibid.

Chapter 2. Big Ideas in Small Packages: The Etudes and Preludes

36   "sketches, beginnings of": Quoted in Samson, *Cambridge Companion to Chopin*, 133.

Chapter 3. The Music for Piano and Orchestra

38   "For these melodies": Quoted in Galatopolous, *Bellini*, 322.

Chapter 6. The Sonatas

69   "yoked four of": Rosen, *Romantic Generation*, 283.
69   "From this musical": Quoted in Rosen, *Romantic Generation*, 283.

Chapter 7. Patriotism and Tragedy: The Polonaises

81   "how unhappy he": Quoted in Siepmann, *Chopin,* 187.

Chapter 8. The Individual Works

90   "the way in": Quoted in Samson, *Cambridge Companion to Chopin*, 257, 326n.
90   "sums up the": Ibid., 270.
90   "the decisive push": Siepmann, *Chopin*, 191.

Selected Bibliography

Eigeldinger, Jean-Jacques. *Chopin: Pianist and Teacher*. Cambridge, UK: The Cambridge University Press, 1986.

Eisler, Benita. *Chopin's Funeral*. New York: Vintage Books, 2003.

Galatopolous, Stelios. *Bellini: Life, Times, Music*. London: Sanctuary Publishing, 2002.

Orga, Ates. *The Illustrated Lives of the Great Composers: Chopin*. London: Midas Press, 1976. Reprint, London: Omnibus Books, 1983.

Rosen, Charles. *The Romantic Generation*. Cambridge MA: Harvard University Press, 1995.

Samson, Jim, ed. *The Cambridge Companion to Chopin*. Cambridge, UK: The Cambridge University Press, 1992.

Schonberg, Harold C. *The Great Pianists*. New York: Simon and Schuster, 1963. Reprint, New York: Fireside Books, 1987.

Siepmann, Jeremy. *Chopin: The Reluctant Romantic*. Boston: Northeastern University Press, 1995.

Szulc, Tad. *Chopin in Paris: The Life and Times of the Romantic Composer*. New York: Da Capo Press, 1998.

CD Track Listing

All performances on the enclosed CD are by pianist Idil Biret from her recording of Chopin's complete piano music on Naxos.

1. Etude in A-flat major, op. 25, no. 1 (2:42)
   Naxos 8.554528

2. Etude in E minor, op. 25, no. 5 (3:50)
   Naxos 8.554528

3. Prelude in E minor, op. 28, no. 4 (2:25)
   Naxos 8.554536

4. Prelude in F-sharp minor, op. 28, no. 8 (2:00)
   Naxos 8.554536

5. Prelude in F major, op. 28, no. 23 (0:54)
   Naxos 8.554536

6. Prelude in A minor, op. 28, no. 2 (2:15)
   Naxos 8.554536

7. Waltz in C-sharp minor, op. 64, no. 2 (3:58)
   Naxos 8.554539

8. Nocturne in D-flat major, op. 27, no. 2 (6:18)
   Naxos 8.554045

9. Finale of Sonata no. 2 in B-flat minor, op. 35 (1:42)
   Naxos 8.554533

10. Polonaise in F-sharp minor, op. 44 (11:47)
    Naxos 8.554534

11. Berceuse in D-flat major, op. 57 (4:46)
    Naxos 8.554527

12. Scherzo no. 3 in C-sharp minor, op. 39 (8:29)
    Naxos 8.554538

13. Mazurka no. 15 in C major, op. 24, no. 2 (2:13)
    Naxos 8.554529

14. Mazurka no. 21 in C-sharp minor, op. 30, no. 4 (4:33)
    Naxos 8.554529

15. Mazurka no. 27 in E minor, op. 41, no. 2 (3:17)
    Naxos 8.554530

16. Ballade no. 4 in F minor, op. 52 (12:19)
    Naxos 8.554527